Living
Successfully with
Screwed-Up
People

Other books by Elizabeth B. Brown

Sunrise Tomorrow: Coping with a Child's Death
The Joy Choice

Living Successfully with Screwed-Up People

Elizabeth B. Brown

Revell

a division of Baker Publishing Group
Grand Rapids, Michigan

© 1999 by Elizabeth B. Brown

Published by Revell
a division of Baker Publishing Group
P. O. Box 6287, Grand Rapids, MI 49516-6287
www.revellbooks.com

New paperback edition published 2010

Printed in the United States of America

Library of Congress Cataloging-in-Publication Data
Brown, Elizabeth B.
    Living successfully with screwed-up people / Elizabeth B. Brown.
        p.   cm.
    Originally published: Grand Rapids, Mich. : F.H. Revell, c1999. With new introd.
    Includes bibliographical references.
    ISBN 978-0-8007-3288-2 (pbk.)
    1. Interpersonal relations—Religious aspects—Christianity. I. Title.
BV4597.52.B76 2009
248.4—dc22   2009036470

13   14   15   16   17   14   13

To those *many very special* people in my life who have
shown me the meaning of grace
To those *few very difficult* people who have taught me how
to "love in spite of"
And, especially, to my beloved husband, Paul,
whose balance and unconditional love
help me appreciate the miracles in every relationship—the
loving and supportive and the challenging

Contents

Introduction
to the 2010 Edition

Are you searching for lifelines to keep you balanced in a relationship with a person who is driving you crazy? In this relationship, would you describe yourself as too often simmering, angry, hurt, or exploding? Is there little consideration for your feelings, your needs? Do you steel yourself against something awful happening—the unfair, without-any-justice-thing that time after time knocks you over? Do you struggle to control your response when a shoe drops, a remark slams, blame points, or criticism flies? Then you need this book!

We know that chaos sits on the throne in difficult relationships. Confusion reigns. Remember the times you may have asked yourself: *Should I get out? Should I quit my job, leave my home, stay away at holidays?* Perhaps the maybes ran pell-mell in your thoughts: *Maybe if I had not said that, maybe I am guilty, maybe there is no hope.* You felt discouraged when the inside whys began: *Why am I left out? Why am I put down, unaccepted, disrespected, unloved, unappreciated?* You ask despondently: *Why do I let myself be hurt?* The answer is simple: YOU CARE.

You care because you are not a quitter. You care because this is a family member, or friend, or coworker. You care because you know in the long run if you can survive the relationship, it is best for the big picture. You care because of commitment, because of children, because they are your offspring, because you are a decent person who believes in getting along and not deserting the ship or skipping out when things get tough.

Sharon cared, but she wanted *change*. She was burdened by the attitude of a family member with whom she couldn't get along but did not want to disconnect. As she listened to people talk about their loss in the grief seminar I was leading, she determined her grief was different: *If your spouse dies, your house burns down, your child commits suicide, you have to move on. You can't do anything about your situation. But my mother needs to be overhauled. She wants to control everything I do. She doesn't like my friends, hates my husband, thinks I feed the kids junk. She is just a pain in my life. She* could *change—and she should—*then *I could be happy.* Her comment was the impetus for this book.

This young woman thought her situation was unique. Surely, she should have recognized that the two hundred people in the seminar were there because they, too, were struggling, wanting what they did not have and wishing things could be different. They did not have to move on just because their loss was permanent. In fact, in divorce, which today is a common loss, one of the divorcees is usually struggling with anger and hurts ten years after D-day. The statistics are as damning for those who lose a child or spouse. Loss of anything—especially loss of expectations and dreams in our relationships—requires new vision, goals, and courage.

A doctor telephoned me from an airport where he had been stranded during a storm. Bored, he went to the bookstore searching for a good read. He was drawn by the original cover of *Living Successfully with Screwed-up People*—a man being turned like a screw. "That was exactly what I felt," he said. "I have been trying so hard to stay in my second marriage. For four years I have been to counselors, asked for help, and was about to call it quits. All those years of seeking help did not put it together for me like your book did in the three hours it took me to read it. I was blaming everything on my wife—and, believe me, she deserves the blame, but I am part of the picture. Thanks for some major lifelines and lots of hope. Bottom line: I'm not going to end up a screwed-up person also."

My insight into difficult relationships changed radically following a seven-year-old daughter's death. LeeAnne was jovial, bouncing, dancing, and hugging on Friday—and dead on Monday from a Reye's type virus. She had developed Type 1 diabetes (also called juvenile diabetes) at age two. Diabetes in a child is tough, and though it had nothing to do with her death, the disease had abused her with radical swings in her blood sugar levels. Her friends didn't criticize when her mood swung from giggly to morose as her blood sugar plunged. They would come to her teacher—or us—and say, "LeeAnne needs something to eat so she can feel good."

I was grateful that their caring made it possible for Lee-Anne to treat her diabetes as a challenge, not a handicap. As I studied the many ways others' actions had stabilized her life, I was overcome by a vision of a very difficult person in my life. Though I loved this family member, her actions caused tremendous chaos and turmoil. I envisioned this person as a child like my little daughter—a jovial, bouncing, dancing, and hugging child—who was handicapped. Though I thought her role was to nurture and support me, the reality was that God needed *me* to love *her* so that, though she might always be *challenged*, she had the possibility of not being *handicapped*.

Sometimes just getting a new vision can change how you cope. The insight changed my life—and filled me with gratitude and caring for the very challenging person whose same actions drove me crazy before. Still, I needed lifelines and handles. I needed things to tell myself when I was coping with off-the-wall events. It is not adequate to think that just because we love all will be well. Believing that this too shall pass may be comforting, but emotions still beg for attention when hurtful behavior pushes our buttons. We will discuss the many issues that swirl around *Living Successfully with Screwed-up People*, such as how to keep out of harm's way if someone is stepping on your foot, when enough is enough, and how to forgive without becoming trampled.

Be assured that it is possible to live, work, and coexist with a difficult person. Together, let's seek the keys to living with purpose and joy, regardless of the challenging people in our lives.

1

Put On Your Glasses

Vision is the starting point of victory.

At a soccer game I stood next to a young man who asked me a question that disturbs many of us: Why do I have the most difficult relationship problems with the people I love?

David did not know I was writing a book on relationships or that I address the question he asked in seminars across the country. He just needed an ear, and I was standing next to him, watching fifteen-year-olds play ball, when his query popped out. I asked him what he thought the answer is.

"I don't know," he said. "It just seems the very people we care most about are the ones that give us the most grief."

He was right: Friends and family can be pains—in the heart. Too often close relationships are better at causing demolition than building. Perhaps that is why suicides increase tenfold during the holidays. Having traveled over the hills and through the valleys to grandmother's house, many of us leave wondering why we went to such efforts to be put through the wringer by someone in our own family. Times together, which should refresh, energize, and heal old wounds, often exacerbate the pain and cause new lesions. The sad truth is that families fight, husbands and wives attack, neighbors feud, friends and coworkers criticize, and children rebel.

The young man at the soccer game was experiencing an undeniable crisis as his expectations butted heads with reality. He believed, as most of us do, that his friends and family should support, encourage, and appreciate him; instead, two of the people he was closest to caused him tremendous anguish as they pointed out his shortcomings, the best choices for his life, ways to be a better person, and the reasons his dreams were not possible. Mere acquaintances encouraged him; his own flesh and blood cut him into pieces. The ones who should care, hurt; the ones who had no obligation to care, affirmed. What was wrong?

You may be in the same situation. Strangers aren't your problem. The person who is driving you nuts is someone you love or someone whose encouragement and appreciation you need. You are shattered by close friends, family, or people you work with every day.

This is how I answered David: "I know you are confused and discouraged, but you are at the most exciting point of understanding relationships! Put on your glasses! You need improved vision to discover the freedom and joy you only imagined were possible within your difficult relationships."

New Vision

I knew David would better understand the concept of putting on his glasses if I shared with him the story of a young woman who expected me to give her a quick fix for her predicament. Sarah too was at a low point in a relationship. "I came to your seminar because I need help," she explained. "You keep saying I must see what I have instead of focusing on what I don't have in a difficult relationship, but your example of a person who moves on after a major life catastrophe isn't valid for me. People who go through a tragedy that involves great loss have no choice but to accept what has happened and move on. After all, if your house burns up, your health is gone, or someone you love dies, what can you do?

"My mother is my grief, and she lives with me, criticizing everything I do. Tragedy survivors have to deal finally with their reality. They can't change the situation. But I could leave—or better yet, if my mother would lighten up, we could enjoy each other. Do you have help for my problem?"

New vision was my answer. When Merlin the Magician flew with the soon-to-be-king Arthur above the forest in Walt Disney's *The Sword and the Stone*, Arthur saw the land below him with a new vision. Merlin, wanting his protégé's aerial view to provide insights about the atrocity of war, questioned Arthur about what he saw. Arthur cried out, "I see everything so clearly. There are no drawn lines and boundaries on the land. People fight over arbitrary lines they draw on a map when all we need to do is move the lines in our minds."

I asked Sarah if she would fly, so to speak, as did Arthur, over her messed-up relationship. Aerial vision would help her see that there were no arbitrary lines, triggers, or buttons—*unless she allowed them.* No one could control her unless she allowed the control. She needed to understand that it takes partners to develop a screwed-up relationship. With new vision she would see not only the wrong actions on the part of the screwed-up mother who caused chaos in her

> Aerial vision clears away illusion: Wrong actions are wrong; wrong responses to wrong actions are equally wrong.

life, but her own responses and actions that were adding to the problem. With aerial vision she would fly above the fray and see that it takes two people to keep conflict and control alive.

Sarah's problem was not so different from that of David or of someone who experiences great loss. Each situation is laden with unhappiness; each causes longing for what is not there—acceptance and happiness—each person has important choices to make. When we face problems, we are at a critical junction. Our choices will either keep us from being pulled into the muck and mire of a screwed-up relationship or cause us to sink as we fight the whirlpools spinning off the person we find difficult or off the longing for what we are not going to have. We need to see and understand clearly our present predicament to discern what is possible for the future.

Unfortunately, difficult relationships are like swamps. In a swamp your vision is obscured by vines, alligators, snakes, and mosquitoes. Screwed-up relationships are mired in muck and swamped by chaos. So much is going on, you don't know how to find solid ground. About the time you begin to wade out of a period of turmoil, a snake bites or an alligator threatens and you lose your footing. Your struggle for self-preservation so occupies you that you are unable to analyze the source of your problems. You wonder: Am I responsible for all the chaos? Or is the person who drives me crazy truly messed up and responsible for the havoc?

> The swamp bottom is often the beginning of renewal.

When your vision is obscured by the swamp, you need to see your relationship with a challenging person from a different perspective. Aerial vision allows you to see

- the possibilities
- the improbabilities
- the impossible

With aerial vision you can see that the yardstick by which you measure relationships is far more rigid and unforgiving for those close to you than is the stretchable line you use to judge outsiders. That is why we can find the capriciousness of a stranger or acquaintance entertaining, but the same behavior in a friend or family member is potential fodder for arguments. What is amusing in someone we hold at a distance is an idiosyncrasy that we want to expel from the person we care about, work with, or live beside. The closer we are to someone, the more we expect from him. We are disappointed, confused, angry, hurt, encouraged, happy, or ecstatic in our relationships according to how close our expectations meet reality. Realistic vision frees us to relate to those close to us with the same objectivity we are able to use with those who touch our life but are not intertwined with our needs.

This reminded David of a difficult person he works with. He said, laughingly, "There's a man in my office who drives everyone crazy with his ranting and raving. He is always going bonkers about some issue, crisis, or potential earthquake. I just laugh. I really like the guy."

"Would you want to live with him?" I asked.

"No way! No more than that woman at your seminar liked living with her nagging mother. His son works at our company too and is always embarrassed or picking up the pieces after his dad has blown someone out of the water with his negative comments."

A light turned on in David's thoughts. "I consider this guy funny, even though he is a pain in the rear to a lot of people at work, yet I go bonkers over some of the things that the two people close to me do that aren't nearly as bad. Am I using a different yardstick to measure the people close to me?"

Healthy Relationships

When we understand why we enjoy one off-the-wall person but feel threatened by another, we will have turned a key that will help us, like David, relate without chaos in all our relationships. Respecting differences is crucial to getting along with people. You could share stories of people you cherish, even admire, who think, act, react, and choose differently than you. Perhaps you seek advice from those who offer different slants. You laugh with people who are out to lunch and don't have all their oars in the water. Like meals, people and relationships would be boring if they were all the same.

David laughed at his coworker's idiosyncrasies. He did not feel responsible for his coworker's choices nor threatened by his actions or advice. He didn't need the man's approval or affirmation. He was able to separate himself from his coworker's conduct, and as a result he could enjoy, rather than spin off from, his behavior. His objectivity was joined with caring, which helped him rein in his tendency to correct. This objectivity allowed him to view the coworker as responsible for his own actions. Objectivity in healthy relationships encourages each person to be responsible for his own choices and actions and the consequences of them.

The Foundation Blocks of Healthy Relationships

1. Respect
2. Accepting personal responsibility for one's behavior
3. Allowing others to bear the consequences of their behavior
4. Caring without enabling

Finding the Way Out of the Swamp

You, like David and Sarah, can learn ways to appreciate—even enjoy—the person whose challenging behavior and idiosyncrasies currently drive you nuts. *Living Successfully with Screwed-Up People* is a how-to of ways to stay afloat, set limits, and build a safety net to pull you out of the negative patterns in which you are ensconced.

When you are caught in the spin-offs of ailing relationships, you need a new perspective. When you feel like you're sinking because of the breakdowns in communication that thrive in unhealthy relationships, grab hold of the lifelines. This book will show you how. It will give you a gauge by which you discern:

- key indicators of a healthy relationship
- signs of malfunctioning
- techniques to judge who is responsible for what part of the malfunctioning
- healthy ways to cope and change

For easy reference, the lifelines I identify are summarized at the end of each chapter.

Turning a toxic relationship into a healthy one requires hard work and a new vision. You can't change your situation if you fail to see the problems and the options. Aerial vision brings the needed insight. It separates you from the relationship chaos so your insights can free you from the stranglehold of difficult relationships.

You may want to try the following exercise that I recommend to people struggling in a skewed relationship. These six questions will jump-start your efforts to unscrew difficult relationship problems. As you read through *Living Successfully with Screwed-Up People*, write your notes or insights in a notebook. Put in it your answers to these questions.

1. What emotional tornadoes does the difficult person in your life spin off?
2. How do you react to the screwed-up person in your life?
3. How does your difficult person react to your reactions?
4. If the other person is the problem, are you growing unhealthy actions and reactions in response to him or her?
5. Are you the screwed-up person driving others to reactive behavior?
6. How do others react to your actions and responses?

Refer back to your answers as you read through this book. Jot down the insights you gain that will help you deal with the difficult person in your life. The goal is freedom, and freedom from any form of captivity requires commitment and hard work.

Being Willing to Change

Relationships that are screwed up cause a lot of pain. You need lifelines to pull out of the whirlpools of harmful and hurtful patterns that develop in unhealthy relationships. If you are just beginning to twist, now is the time to reverse your patterns. It will take far less work now than if you wait until later.

> Relationship low points can be hope points.

But if you are already at the bottom in your relationship, lost in a quagmire, take heart, you can reverse the patterns. Often it takes hitting bottom to shatter the illusions and fantasy around a challenged relationship. The bottom can be the beginning of renewal. When you are down, feeling there is no more use, the only way to go is up to a world of possibilities—if you determine to continue with the relationship. Low points can be hope points.

The question for you, as for David and Sarah, is, Do you really want to bring about positive change in your negative relationships? If so, *you* must be willing to change *first*. *Unless you change first, it is unlikely your relationship will do anything but sink deeper into distress.*

> It takes only one person to change a relationship.

Reactive behavior rarely brings positive change. Change in your screwed-up person is far more likely when he recognizes that there is something different about you. Change causes surprise. Those around ask, "Why are you so different?" That's a hope point! Your change may be a stimulus for change in others. It is impossible to continue the same type of interaction if one of the parties has metamorphosed his or her actions and responses.

Having Realistic Expectations

Perhaps you are hoping and waiting for that difficult person in your life to start doing things differently. Maybe you believe that if your difficult person changes, he won't be so offensive to others, will be more fun to be with, and will like himself more. Maybe you are right. But your expectations may be unrealistic.

Let's just assume that some of your desires for the relationship may be as unreal as the husband who wants his stressed-by-kids-and-a-job wife to be a sex goddess on demand. Without his help, she is a Cinderella in ashes. What he wants and what he has may be two different things, yet the potential is there for his dreams to be fulfilled—at least to some degree. His new vision will have to include the reality that, like the fairy godmother, he is a catalyst in the process that will produce a relationship that meets his needs—a healthy family—and a "goddess."

Inga had to adjust her expectations. "My extended family was definitely my problem. They all live busy lives, so periodically to be together we take turns having family dinners. People show up megalate or not at all. Some come and stay a few minutes before leaving to go to something else 'important,' but few bother to call before the dinner to tell the hostess of conflicts. Of course, the excuses are semilegitimate—kids have schedule conflicts; they need to help a neighbor; they are so tired; they forgot. We would be more gracious with perfect strangers."

Inga stewed over the situation. Her posturing and pontificating did no good. Appealing to courtesy didn't bring change. The same patterns continued. I asked her how she handled the problem to keep from spinning off into anger, resentment, and hurt.

"I decided these times were important to me. They provided an opportunity for family closeness and if I complained and nagged, the times together would become sour times, rather than fun, and the opportunity would close. So I shut my mouth and changed my attitude."

Inga couldn't change people by nagging, but she could make adjustments so that she could relax and enjoy the family that came together. When she was the hostess, she changed from sit-down dinners to buffets so there were no table settings and it didn't matter how many came. She served foods that could be eaten hot or cold and could be refrigerated as leftovers. She chose to be grateful for the time together with whoever came. Their coming was a gift. She thanked the ones who came, and when family members who missed the time together called after the evening with excuses, she enthusiastically said, "We had such a good time, but we sure missed you!"

Each chapter of *Living Successfully with Screwed-Up People* addresses the how-to question. The answers or suggestions, like Inga's, work. They have been meticulously researched and studied. Patterns can be reversed. It is possible to regain control of thoughts and restructure a life that abuse has tumbled into chaos through the years. People can change. *You* can change.

We will talk about expectations—realistic and unrealistic, and the disappointment that can stem from them as we move through this book together. A baseline, a starting point, is necessary to determine *where you are* so you can set realistic goals for *where you want to be*. Use this two-minute test to pinpoint the health of your relationship and the health of your coping techniques.

The Clear Vision Test is a step toward a stronger, renewed, and vital relationship. It is a gauge by which you can determine whether your actions and responses to a difficult person are:

- healthy
- challenged
- screwed up

Clear Vision Test

Study the list below. Rank each statement according to how closely it describes you and your challenging relationship. Then add your points and compare the total with the scale at the end.

1 = never feel this
2 = sometimes feel this
3 = quite often feel this

1. I stew and seethe in silence *before* our times together.
2. I worry about and anticipate difficulties and chaos that will come *after* most of our times together.
3. I feel manipulated, intimidated, and controlled most of the time.
4. I feel unappreciated most of the time.
5. I feel I am always having to defend myself.
6. I feel overwhelming guilt after our being together.
7. I feel like "something is eating me alive."
8. My conversations with others often spin off the negative actions or reactions I have to this person.
9. I seem unable to control my anger, resentment, or hurt when we are together or after we have been together.
10. I feel like I will never be able to measure up to what is expected.
11. I feel like a loser when I express my ideas, needs, or beliefs.
12. I try to plan out my actions and reactions before we get together.
13. I fantasize about getting even.
14. I fantasize about getting out.
15. I feel I must protect someone other than myself from harm—physical or psychological—caused by the difficult person.

16. I long to help this person change so he or she will be happier.
17. I long to help this person change so I will be happier.
18. I explode at the most unexpected times.
19. I do not feel happy most of the time.
20. I don't like me most of the time.
21. Most of the time I long for our relationship to be different.

If your score is:

21: Your relationship is normal and healthy.

22–34: Your relationship is skewing.

35–63: Your relationship and your reactions to it are unhealthy.

Be encouraged. If the test indicates that there is a problem, you can seek solutions.

If you are tired of fighting, tired of always being put down, tired of feeling like a spare part, hurt, discouraged, blue, and let down, read on. David and Sarah *did* change their relationships—for the better. You can too! Don't be discouraged. Grab the lifelines. *It takes only one person to change a relationship.*

Lifelines

- Aerial vision clears away illusion: Wrong actions are wrong; wrong responses to wrong actions are equally wrong.
- The swamp bottom is often the beginning of renewal.
- Relationship low points can be hope points.
- It takes only one person to change a relationship.

2

When the Pressure Is On

Enough is enough.

Hearing the lilt of her canary's song, a fastidious house-keeper's attention was drawn to the bird's cage, which she saw immediately needed cleaning. She decided that it would be easy to clean the cage bottom with her new vacuum cleaner. Disregarding the frantic bird, she stuck the vacuum wand into the cage and was occupied with her task when the doorbell rang. Startled, she raised the wand, and the nervous canary was sucked in. Alarmed and expecting the worst, the woman quickly turned off the cleaner and opened it to retrieve the bird. To her relief, he appeared okay. He was stunned but otherwise none the worse for the experience. So she put him back on his perch, where he sat, songless.

Too often that's what happens when we cope with screwed-up people: We are sucked in, and if we do not understand our predicament and options, especially when the pressure is on, we remain in a state of disequilibrium. We may not appear to be affected by our experience, but in reality we've changed. Our song is lost as we swing back and forth on our perch, going nowhere.

Recognizing the Problem

Pressure in a difficult relationship is the result of one simple fact: You care. If you didn't care, it would not make any difference what someone did or did not do. It would be irrelevant. Because you care, you are defensive. Not caring, you could stand back, assess the problem, ascertain the possibilities, and devise a plan for successful survival. You know what you want, you understand what you need, and you long to move toward your goals. But the externals—friends, family, commitments, duties, and responsibilities—conflict with your objectives. You don't have a song because it is too hard to sing when inside you're moaning: I can't handle this. What am I to do?

Caring makes you feel pulled in different directions. It's like being directionless. *It's not that you are lost; it's that you do not know which way to go.* Like the bird, you are perched, apprehensive about the unknown, wanting to sing but too afraid or angry to do so. You fear that if you do for your SUP what caring demands, you will lose friends, offend family, hurt others, be accused of irresponsibility, or be held up as a bad example. The canary was unable to figure out what happened to him, so he didn't know what to do to prevent it from happening again. Fortunately, you are not a bird. You can figure out what to do to live with a vacuum hose in your cage, because you recognize the source of the suction and understand the end result of being pulled in.

Good mental health depends on discernment that assesses the situation, determines options, and moves on, even though you care. Don't allow the pressure to force you into compliance with behavior that:

- is wrong
- goes against your beliefs
- would squash someone's spirit
- is immoral

When you are feeling pressured, ask yourself, Am I complying because I feel family pressure to do what they think is right, not what I want for my life? Am I complying because I feel this is the best option for my long-term good and for those for whom I am responsible? Is this best, even though it may not feel good now? Am I complying because I feel I have no choice? Am I doing something I feel is wrong morally, ethically, or legally? The answers will guide you in either moving on with your commitment or stopping to analyze your situation further.

> When the pressure is on, you are not necessarily lost, you just don't know which way to go.

Handling the Pressure

If you want to handle the pressure in and surrounding difficult relationships, self-control is essential. Four ingredients help make self-control possible: humor, prayer, work, and friends. Humor brings objectivity, prayer grounds you in hope, work keeps you busy, and friends bring normalcy back into your focus. It is important for you to remember: You can't do it alone, but when you are alone, humor helps. Laughter diffuses a potentially explosive or implosive situation.

In a class as we were talking about relationship pressures, a forty-year-old man spoke up about his work experience. James shared, "My boss, Fred, was a tyrant. He came in to work screaming every day of the fifteen years I worked for him. He ate people alive as he exploded, 'It's not you. It's the mistake I am yelling at!' That's hard to believe when he is demanding, 'What kind of idiot would do this? Where is your common sense?' That feels personal. I stayed for two reasons—first, the money. I was overcompensated for the posi-

> You can't do it alone, but when you are alone, humor helps.

tion I held, but not when you added in the guff I had to put up with. The second reason I stayed was bottom line—I cared. I knew he needed my help, even if he didn't act like it.

"Yet working for Fred was like being in a washing machine. You never knew when the agitation was going to get to you. So when I got to the point I couldn't handle the ridicule and control anymore, I would say to Fred, 'Fred, I'm already over-compensated for this managerial position, but your attitude is so hard to handle that if you want me to stay, you have to up my salary.' When I left for another job, there were only three of the original group of twenty-seven who were still with the production company. I worked successfully, putting up with a real jerk, because I knew how much I was willing to endure for the salary and benefits—and because I didn't need Fred's appreciation to know I made a difference."

In chapter 4, "Get Off the Fence," we will discuss the need to decide whether you are going to stay or quit your difficult relationship. You may have tried to settle that question in your mind, yet, when the pressure is on, you must ask, Can I handle this any longer?

The pressure is real. How can you quit your job when your family needs the money? How could you leave your husband when you have a family to raise? How do you live your own life without rejecting your parents' demands? How do you handle the sister-brother pressure to conform to their mold? Pressure builds as siblings are pleading, parents are blaming, or the kids are crying. You feel songless because it does matter to you what others think. You do care about what happens. The people who have power to exert pressure are important to you. So how do you find your song again when you are still in the cage with the potential for being sucked back into the vacuum cleaner?

I asked James to be specific about what he did to stay without being pulled into the fray when the pressures built and tensions escalated. He listed five simple steps.

1. Recognize what causes the tension.
2. Ascertain your options.
3. Consider the cost.
4. Know your limits.
5. Own your choice.

Let's think together about these five steps and how they affect our self-control. We can live victoriously in almost any situation if we can control our thoughts and actions. Understanding what's going on may encourage us to consciously think through our behavior, rather than merely act on automatic pilot. The chaos in difficult relationships makes *automatic responses* a surefire disaster.

Steps to Self-Control

Recognize What Causes the Tension

Life within a difficult relationship is like being on a wave. The tensions escalate, peak, flatten, and then begin to escalate again. Smooth sailing is always short-lived. Successfully handling the tension lies in knowing that the waves are always in motion, as opposed to assuming, since the water is smooth today, it will be smooth tomorrow. Pressure to comply may become nearly unbearable when we believe:

• we are the only one our screwed-up person attacks
• what we do may save the day
• our way is right and her way is wrong
• the demands go against our ethics
• we don't want to do it her way

We need to get over it. Being a grown-up is dependent on our fully understanding the reality: Our compliance is our choice. No one can control someone else (unless the person being controlled allows it). No one controls you—unless you allow that control. Sure, she can put the screws to your head, but ultimately what you do within the circumstances of your life is dependent on what you allow and how much you are willing to sacrifice to have things your own way or to win approval. Whenever there are disagreements in relationships with difficult people, the pressure is enormous and the potential for loss always present.

Understanding why you feel pressure, and that ultimately what you do with the pressure is your choice, begins to open your eyes to your options. Knowing your options prepares you for the next encounter—which, when coping with difficult people, is inevitable.

> No one controls you—unless you allow the control.

In any pressure-loaded situation, you must decide your course. Talk it out. The problem will not resolve itself. It will only get worse as time goes on and you, by your silence, comply. Don't tell me the obvious: I don't talk to the boss because he is the boss; he doesn't listen; he shouts; he'll fall apart; I'll be fired. If you intend to change the pressure and its power in your life, you must talk about your options and state your limits and boundaries to the person who has the ability to bring about change. James told his boss what he had to have to stay as office manager. He said it honestly, quietly, and without rage, threats, or blame. That meant his boss had to make a decision and James had to accept the consequences. When you set your limits, you too must be willing to accept the consequences.

Ascertain the Options

A good or, in some cases, a tolerable relationship is the result of hard work. It is dependent on your being very realistic about the situation. To determine your options, you must quit rationalizing or justifying. Healthy relationships are built on realism, not fantasy. James could survive a hellion (his word) as an employer because he was realistic. The boss had no tact, no idea of how his words stung, and no sense of team play. He was a control freak. And James determined his options were either play the way the boss wants to play or get another job.

James saw his situation realistically. "It was hard to watch Fred make decisions I knew would potentially kill the production company or turn away a contract that could help it grow. I would tell him what I honestly thought and then leave it alone. Sometimes that got so hard to watch that I would leave the office to get away and regain my perspective. He owned the company. He could sell it, kill it, or flush it down the tubes. If I could not live with his choices, I could leave."

But often logic skews in difficult relationships because people justify or rationalize a screwed-up person's off-the-wall behavior instead of labeling it for what it is—wrong. When false assumptions are the foundation of interactions, the relationship built on them will be shaky. Rationalizations and justifications create such an unstable foundation.

As you read the following statements, think about your own difficult relationship. Are you using any of these rationalizations as justifications? If so, you are limiting your options and your ability to act on your own. Consider the fact that follows each statement.

1. My SUP's terrible childhood is why she acts so irrationally. *A person's choices, not his or her childhood, determine actions.*
2. My SUP needs me to make him happy. *Happiness is his inside job.*
3. My SUP can't make it without me. *This is codependency! an unhealthy relationship!*
4. It is the wrong I do that causes my SUP to be so crazy. *Each person is responsible for his or her own actions and reactions.*
5. I never want to do anything my SUP would not approve. *Healthy relationships are built on negotiation and compromise, not on approval based on performance.*
6. I couldn't survive without my SUP. *This shows your unhealthy self-esteem. Get counseling help.*
7. No matter what my SUP does, I will support her. *Wrong acts are wrong. You can care for and love someone without condoning behavior that hurts others or is illegal.*
8. I worry about what my SUP thinks about my choices. *Care? Yes. Worry? No!*

9. I know if I just try hard enough, my SUP will appreciate me. *If he doesn't appreciate you now, he never will. His care is a gift he can give or withhold.*
10. I fight with my SUP all the time. *Constant fighting is indicative of an unhealthy relationship.*
11. If I stand up to my SUP, she will end our relationship. *A relationship is healthy when it is a partnership, not a game of domination or submission.*

Consider the Cost

The reason pressure is felt in difficult relationships is that going against the will of a screwed-up person will cost you. The overall benefits of any situation must be weighed against the losses. The pressure is on because you care and you don't want to lose a relationship you value but you also don't want to lose your ability to govern your own life. James stayed and willingly submitted to his boss because the paycheck justified the anguish. When he no longer considered the salary enough justification for the anguish, the pressure seemed overpowering and he left. Every path has its cost. Make your decision and then don't fret over the choice. Wallowing in self-pity just makes it worse, keeping your emotions bouncing off the fence you are straddling.

Know Your Limits

James's eyes were open. He knew his boss was probably never going to change; he knew he would have to be the one to bend if he wanted to stay in the job. He also knew how far he was willing to bend. Knowing your limits makes it easier to own your choice. If you feel like a gun is to your head, determine why the gun is there, what your options are, how long you can stand for it to stay pointed at you, and what you are going to do about it.

Own Your Choice

The key ingredient for reducing pressure in your difficult relationships is you. When you own what you are willing to do, commit, give, or limit within your relationship, your choice sets the boundaries and consequences. Choice involves evaluation of the cost and the options, then determining the best course of action. These, in turn, cause the pressure to dissipate, like air seeping out of a torn tire.

Be bold. Determine your course. Courage and resolve undergird your decisions when you act on what you know to be true. Give yourself time to assess the situation. Take a breather. You don't want to rush your decisions when under pressure, but you do need to know that if you don't steer your own boat, someone else will be happy to steer it for you.

What Is Your Choice?

Recognizing his accent was not local, I asked a taxi driver in Texas where he was from originally. He responded, "Yugoslavia" and began telling us of the ethnic cleansing problem going on in his country that had forced him to leave seven years before.

I suggested, "The change must have been difficult."

"Not really," was his quick reply. "My choice was keeping things as they were (staying on the perch) or keeping my life."

Put like that, the option is easy—life. That seems to be the same choice each of us has as we cope within a difficult situation. We can change when the pressure is on and we find ourselves sucked in, or something will die—the relationship, our zest, or our *self*. What is your choice?

Lifelines

- When the pressure is on, you are not necessarily lost; you just don't know which way to go.
- You can't do it alone, but when you are alone, humor helps.
- No one controls you—unless you allow the control.

3

Who Is Screwed Up?

Screwed-up people are ordinary people who cause hurricanes in your emotions.

I began to recognize the need for someone to write a book about coping within difficult relationships when I found much of the question-and-answer portion of my seminars and retreats moving from grief issues to the difficulties of coping with challenging relationships. I saw a logical application of all I had learned about coping with high-stress times caused by major turmoil—disease, death, divorce—to our coping with the chaos generated from living in challenging relationships.

I shared with my audiences the idea of writing a book about screwed-up people. They nodded and laughed knowingly. "We could give you some stories!" they shouted. Then, following the lectures, participants came to talk privately—some with heads bowed, some with a stiff, angry demeanor, some with a penetrating sadness—about life with Momma, a boss that made Simon Legree look saintly, a child who was born smoking cigars, teachers from hell, sisters and brothers who hated them. It wasn't that these people who shared their stories were different, had off-the-wall ideas, or had chosen different lifestyles from the norm. Each could have been a neighbor, friend, or even a family member. But they all said things like, I hurt . . . I am never appreciated . . . Nothing ever works . . . I can't please . . . The only way to get along is to say, "Yes, ma'am!"

Chaos, control, and pain were the common threads that ran through each life story. Men and women talked about marital bliss changing to doldrums or misery. Parents talked about all they had done for children who now answered them curtly or acted as if they were a bother. Children recalled being told to shut up and keep out of the way. Bosses talked about employees who were disloyal; employees talked about supervisors who treated them like lackeys. Though many of the relationships seemed hopeless, each person wanted to know if the relationship was redeemable. Was it too late to change what seemed like an impossible relationship?

Who Will Change?

I knew I could help. Through counseling with thousands of people across America privately and in seminars, I knew there are lifelines to keep people from drowning in the tension of difficult relationships. There are danger signs that can warn of unhealthy patterns. Choices can be taught that stop actions and reactions from spinning off to warp people and destroy relationships. Sick and shaky relationships can be transformed and revitalized.

I asked, "Do you want to transform the way you interact with the people you label unfair, uncaring, off-base, judgmental, harsh, driven, wimpy, whining, and/or clinging?" All agreed a transformation was needed—in the screwed-up persons! I could not help the people who shouted loudly, "I am not the problem. I'm not the one who is off-the-wall! I'm not the one who treats people like dirt. I'm not the one who is so unfair . . . controlling . . . mean . . . stingy." They saw the problem clearly: "The other person is wrong—not me!" Their vision was one-sided.

> It takes two people to create a screwed-up relationship.

Most relationships don't become screwed up because *one* person is doing it wrong. They become unhealthy because two people spin off each other. Unhealthy relationships require two participants, and at least one must be willing to change before anything can be done that offers the hope of a better relationship.

It's easy to recognize the people who have become victors in difficult relationships. They have realized that changing the other person does not work, so they develop whatever is necessary to find a sense of peace within their difficult relationships and a way to be happy as they handle their responsibilities and commitment.

They ask, "What can I do in this impossible situation?"

The reality is clear: The person who is driving us crazy may never change, but we can change ourselves and the relationship for the better. We can disarm a dysfunctional relationship *by taking control of our own acts.*

When Relationships Are a Mess

People in a screwed-up relationship interact in a way similar to that of a nut and a bolt. In a sense, the two intertwine and together have strength disproportionate to their size. Likewise, people or relationships that are screwed up wrap around the actions and responses of each other, becoming entangled with a disproportionate amount of strength. The slowly built and twisted complexity of the troublesome relationship develops as wrong actions spin off wrong responses.

Psychologists label this twisting process codependency. Our unhealthy actions and responses spin around our interactions with difficult, abusive, troubled, or needy people. These spin-off or spin-around responses—conflict, whining, manipulation, secrecy, and a bagful of compulsive and irregular behaviors—complicate the interactions. Fortunately, screws can be unscrewed, and hurting, hostile relationships can be untangled. First, you must figure out who the difficult person is (that's the easy part!) and how your behavior either exacerbates or defuses the chaos within the relationship (that's the hard part!).

We may hesitate to call another person screwed up. After all, don't we all have flaws? And when we observe people, we find that they are rarely off the wall in every relationship, nor overbearing in all areas. In fact a person may be adored by most people in her world, but in one or a few key relationships, she is definitely a problem.

For our purposes we can say that someone is screwed up in a relationship in which she continuously causes havoc— by choices, actions, and responses that are inappropriate, manipulative, mean, abusive, and so on. Screwed-up people aren't crazy. They are normal people who constantly spin off bad choices, actions, and responses that cause the other person to feel used, abused, controlled, unappreciated, challenged, depressed, incapable, hopeless, or angry. In other words, they cause internal hurricanes.

Difficult people have myopic vision that centers them squarely on their belly button. They are self-centered, self-absorbed, and, often, self-destructive. As they stare inward, their focus is *their* feelings, *their* needs, *their* rights. Their behavior echoes: You don't do enough for me. You hurt me. You failed me. You aren't being fair to me. You should do what I want, the way I know is best. You need me because I am better than you.

The common drive of screwed-up people is for control. They use whatever is necessary to get it: blame, guilt, shame. The victim in the relationship becomes used to bowing, scraping, and begging as his self-esteem is damaged. The screwed-up person is victimized also, as she becomes locked into self-destructive patterns of control.

Stopping the March

Jean Henri Fabre, a French naturalist in the late 1800s, spent his life observing insects and spiders. He wrote simply of what he saw in the gardens and fields near his home, compiling the information and pictures into a ten-volume *Souvenirs Entomologiques*. One of his most noted studies was on processionary caterpillars. These caterpillars follow their leader through the trees, linked head to tail in one great chain, devouring leaves as they march. Fabre placed a group of the insects on the top of a pottery crock. A world of greenery lay within inches of the crock, but the caterpillars, locked into their march, followed blindly, round and round, until days later the march ended in the death of the insects. They did not break the pattern, even though following the same-old-same-old meant death.

You may be locked into a march around screwed-up behaviors just like processionary caterpillars, stuck in the same old ruts and grooves. If you are, don't be discouraged. You aren't a caterpillar. Habits and patterns of behavior are not set in concrete, any more than the pattern of the caterpillars' march was unchangeable. After all, just by moving the caterpillars, Fabre changed their march from the trees to the crock. They marched on, barely missing a step. Your challenge is not just to change your march's location, but to stop the march completely.

The following questions will help you determine if you are marching in the wrong direction in your relationship. Even one yes answer is unhealthy and portends a skewing relationship.

1. Do you base how you feel on what he or she does?
2. Do you worry about whether the person is attentive enough, cares enough, is supportive enough?
3. Does his or her periodic praising of someone else threaten you?
4. Do you store up the wrongs he or she does toward you?
5. Do you finish the statement, "You make me feel . . ." with negatives?
6. Do you feel hampered and controlled by the relationship?
7. Do you constantly worry and fret about your relationship?
8. Are the problems in the relationship eating you alive?
9. Are you overwhelmed with guilt about what you do or don't do?

10. Are you seething over issues that swirl off the other person?
11. Do you feel unappreciated most of the time?
12. Do you feel what you do is futile in the relationship?
13. Do you do things you hate because it is expected of you?
14. Do you resent any time he or she spends helping others?

If you answered yes to any of these questions, you may be forfeiting your power and ability to think, feel, and act independently.

Interdependency is spinning into codependency when relationships exhibit these traits:

- extreme emotional dependency (one person feels she can do nothing without the other person)
- excessive worry and preoccupation (centered around one person's choices)
- constant reactive behavior (one person reacting to what the other does or does not do)
- consuming mental, physical, and emotional energy directed at changing one person

> Interdependency is healthy; dependency is not.

- blame assigned to someone (other than the person committing the acts or having the feelings)
- interactions devoid of laughter and lightness

Knowing whether your chaotic relationship is caused by your unrealistic expectations or by a really toxic person is critical to appreciating what is possible within the relationship. The following exercise will help. Think of the person who is driving you crazy. Check off the traits in the following list of toxic behaviors that the SUP in your relationship manifests. If you check off five or more, you are in a difficult relationship and must be extremely careful not to be sucked into dysfunction. Add up your check marks and fill in the bar below to the number that equals your total score. The closer to 1 your line is, the healthier the relationship; the closer to 20, the more dysfunctional.

Healthy   ⟵—————————————————————⟶   Toxic

1 2 3 4 5 6 7 8 9 10 11 12 13 14 15 16 17 18 19 20

The person who is driving me crazy—

1. Refuses to hear my side of an issue.
2. Turns molehills into mountains and minutiae into significance.
3. Demands the controls.
4. Is self-centered and self-absorbed.
5. Is opinionated—or is self-debasing and self-deprecating with no opinions.
6. Often exhibits self-destructive behavior.
7. Will not listen to reason.
8. Repeats the same negative, fearful, or controlling behavior.
9. Can't be depended on.
10. Feels superior—or inferior.
11. Justifies his or her criticism by superior knowledge, experience, genes, relationship, etc.
12. Does not see the connection between his or her behavior and the chaos it engenders.
13. Encourages conflict.

14. Causes chaos.
15. Blames others.
16. Uses shame and guilt as weapons.
17. Never apologizes for anything or apologizes profusely for everything.
18. Refuses to take responsibility for his or her choices.
19. Controls through manipulation, guilt, money, power, etc.
20. Believes the ends justify the means.

Hanging In

The Romans attached a great deal of importance to the quality of their drinking water. Compliance with their system of aqueducts, holding tanks, and bridges was mandatory for even the smallest town. In the French Cardon valley is one of the most magnificent of these still-standing and usable aqueducts, the Pont du Gard aqueduct, built in the last century B.C. The bridge is an architectural wonder with tiers of arches rising 160 feet from the riverbed and 900 feet in length. The bridge is made of colossal dressed blocks of masonry, some weighing as much as six tons, which were laid without mortar, the courses held together with iron clamps. The stone was lifted into position by block and tackle with goats as auxiliaries and a winch worked by a massive human treadmill.

As you stand hundreds of feet below this magnificent structure, you wonder, *Why has it not collapsed in this modern era of heavy trucks and equipment?* The answer is simple: It remains intact because it is used for nothing but foot traffic. If an eighteen-wheeled tractor trailer were driven across the historic structure, it would crumble in a great cloud of dust and debris.

Relationships that lack an iron-will determination to hang together, like the Roman bridges, may appear to be upright and secure, until they are put under heavy pressure—or under the drip, drip, drip of years of negative interchanges. Years of misuse and abuse make a relationship fragile and vulnerable. Be assured, if anger and resentment lie in your bed, wake with you in the morning, and move with you through the day, you are putting pressure on your relationship that may cause it to crumble.

Although many would say that it is no one's fault when relationships fall apart in our troubled world, the truth is that in every broken or twisted relationship two people are involved and to some extent responsible, and either one can have a tremendous impact on healing and strengthening the broken bonds. You may not have caused a large part of the damage in your relationships, but you are responsible for your role in the entanglement once you recognize there is a problem. *Who* happens to be in your life may be an accident of birth or someone else's doing; what you do with and how you react to those people is your responsibility.

You may be wondering if people can change or, on a more personal level, if it is possible for the screwed-up person in your life or *you* to change. The answer is yes, anyone can change. People are not leopards. They can change their spots, their behaviors, and their way of expressing themselves— with a little help, a lot of desire, time, the right guidance, and effort to adjust expectations that clash with reality. The reality is, however, that no matter what you try or how much effort you exert, the difficult person in your life may always be a problem. Take heart. You have made a sound investment of effort by changing your reactive behavior to proactive behavior. You, at least, are freed from further twisting into dysfunction. A 50 percent return on any investment far exceeds the odds.

Lifelines

- It takes two people to create a screwed-up relationship.
- Interdependency is healthy; dependency is not.

4

Get Off the Fence

The indispensable first step to getting the things you want out of life is this: Decide what you want.

Ed Woods promised himself that he would teach his son Tiger two things: course management and mental toughness. He has written: "One day when Tiger was two, we were on the second hole at Navy Golf Course. He had hit his ball into the trees. 'What are you going to do, Tiger?' The boy replied, 'I can't hit the ball over all these trees, Daddy; they're too tall.'

"'Well, what else could you do?' I asked.

"'I can hit it between those trees, but I've got to keep it down. And there's a big sand twap [*sic*].'

"'OK, what else can you do?' Tiger looked to the left and said, 'I can hit my ball out into the fairway, hit my next shot onto the green, and one-putt for a par.'

"I said, 'Son, that is course management.'"

Tiger went on to manage not only the course but tournaments. On Friday of the 1996 Walt Disney World/Orlando Classic, Tiger read the sports pages and then calmly announced, "Pop, got to shoot 63 today. That's what it will take to get into it."

Pop replied, "So go do it." When he returned later in the day, Pop asked, "Whaddya shoot?" Tiger calmly replied, "Sixty-three."[1]

If you want to heal a damaged relationship, you must do what Tiger Woods did to win his tournaments: *Decide what you want and then determine how to manage your course.* You can't sit halfway on the fence and halfway off. Straddling the fence kills a relationship—or keeps it only halfway alive.

The big question facing every ailing relationship is whether the relationship is worth the effort to keep it going. No one can answer that for someone else. As an outsider, I can suggest that there are three courses to consider when determining whether to stay in or sever a relationship. The first two courses—staying or leaving—come packaged with pluses and minuses that must be seriously evaluated before a clear-cut determination can be made that is either right or wrong. The third course, straddling the fence, however, is always wrong because it messes with the heads of all those touched by the relationship! As in golf, no one wins in a relationship when the effort on anyone's part is halfway, wishy-washy, lukewarm, or unenthusiastic.

Neither choosing to stay nor choosing to leave seems to affect the happiness of most people. For the majority, the relationship continues to be an ongoing, negative experience, regardless of whether they stay or leave, because their decision doesn't get them off the fence emotionally. People seem to be unhappy in the relationship and unhappy out of it, because they cling to the same old stuff in or out. Research has shown that in only 10 percent of couples who divorce do both husband and wife reconstruct happier, fuller lives by the end of the first decade. Only 25 percent of second marriages form a strong enough bond to avoid a second divorce, and even fewer the third go-round. Experience and statistics show that those who fight through the early years of a relationship generally continue to fight throughout its life.[2] By no means does this have to be the reality of your experience if you determine to change the way you relate.

> Straddling the fence is a death sentence for a relationship.

Unfortunately, straddling the fence seems to be the easiest, most frequently chosen course, especially in marriages with children. Sometimes straddling results from fear of involvement, from self-protection, or from an unwillingness to make the necessary compromise and sacrifice. Some stay in a marriage because they want to walk two paths at the same time, having the security of a family and the excitement of dalliances on the side. Others stay with their emotions on guard or as victims, sacrificing conspicuously: Look how much I am doing for you. I am crushed under your feet, repressing who I am for you.

Let me share part of a letter I received. It attests loudly to the fact that though it isn't always the best choice to stay, it is always the best choice, if you do stay, to work through the anger and hurt to find healthy ways to work together.

Dear Elizabeth,

I read your first book with great interest. Though I did not lose a child to death, my parents stayed together for the sake of us kids, which in our case made our home like a death. Everyone tried to stay out of everyone else's hair, do our own things, and not get too close. My parents were constantly at each other's throat behind the bedroom door. Walls are thin and you can hear lots that you shouldn't hear when people are yelling at each other. Hearing anger and resentment on a daily basis was an awful way to grow up.

The tension and bitterness made it apparent to me that my parents had a bad relationship. Their misery showed, and my brother and I suffered from it. My mother played us kids against my dad. My dad stayed away as much as he could and when he was home hid behind work or his paper. He yelled a lot at my brother and just ignored me. Mom tried to compensate for what Dad wasn't doing with us, but when she did anything, she always did it with a sigh, "I have to do it all since your father won't be part of our lives." It hurts to see your mother crying all the time and your father always mad. It made my brother and me feel like we were in the way and a noose around everyone's neck.

I used to pray I could live at a friend's house— or that my parents would leave each other so someone could be happy again. I don't ever remember laughter. Parents who are unhappy with each other often lack warmth. This lack of warmth is felt by their children and affects them in negative ways. My parents did me no favor by showing me that married life could be miserable.

Parents who do decide to stay together owe it to their children to take measures such as family counseling to improve their relationship and ensure they do not convey bitterness to their children. I won't ever "stay" like my folks did. They stayed partway—and left partway. They messed us all up! When I think about my parents and my childhood, I feel sad and sorry.

Making the Choice

Most people would stay if commitment could turn a difficult relationship around. Few of us fear a little hard work if it is guaranteed to bring results. But there are no guarantees, no charts that we can use to measure our sacrifice against progress in moving the relationship forward. So we wail and we wallow in our remorse and pain. We cling, beg, hold on as if our life depended on it. We yell and blame. We stomp out. Wouldn't it be nice if we knew when to hang on tenaciously and when to bail out?

The more bonded we are by time, effort, and commitment, the more painful it is to leave a significant relationship. Giving up feels like failure, like shirking our duties and responsibilities, and like rejection. Most people want to stay, work through their problems, compromise where

they can, and live with what can't be changed. They recognize that no one is perfect, including themselves. They
know about perseverance, overcoming, and grace. They
may even try to love in spite of the imperfections, which
may be the greatest love of all. When they succeed, if they
do so without bitterness and rancor, they become beacons
to the rest of us.

The decision to stay or leave is a lot like an optional
surgery. You wouldn't even consider it if there were not a
problem. You think long and hard about whether having
the surgery would be the best
choice, and you pray for healing. If you choose surgery, it implies the pain is too great and the
hope for regeneration dead. As

> The hope is for a
> new beginning.

the last resort you are willing to endure whatever it is that
must be endured, the discomfort, inconvenience, emotional
upheaval, and new stresses, with the hope that surgery will
give you a new beginning. When you make a decision about
your relationship, it is with the same hope. If you stay or if
you leave, the hope is for a new beginning.

So often when discussing problem relationships, I hear the
cry, "I have no choice." I hear all the justifications: I have to
stay because of the children . . . I can't turn away my brother,
even if he strips us clean, because he's my brother . . . I can't
practice tough love on my kid. He might not make it without
me . . . I stayed home while his career advanced. What can
I do now? I'm stuck . . . I have to do what my parents want
because I owe them so much . . . I can't leave. It's not moral.
I'm forced to stay.

How I wish I had a magic formula that would open the
eyes of those who say, "I have no choice." That's absurd. Of
course you have a choice. The proper question is, Should I
stay or should I leave? People who believe they have no choice

are fence-sitters. And as we've seen, fence-sitting is internal blindness that turns a person into a victim because he or she feels powerless to change the situation. It's far easier to blame someone for your predicament than to hold yourself accountable to make the best you can out of a difficult situation. It's like blaming the golf course when you hit a ball into the rough.

Roy knew he had a choice. He knew to live he had to hang on; to live victoriously he had to let go. He had a health problem, not a relationship crisis, but the lessons he taught while surviving his cancer spoke loudly about the tenacity and perseverance required to struggle through any life battle, regardless of its form. Semicomatose, steadily sliding downhill, Roy's condition left our family and medical team in a quandary trying to balance the time bought by heroic medical measures against the potential suffering. Not expecting an answer, though understanding the necessity for his father-in-law to be a willing partner in the fight, my physician husband repeated his question, "Roy, should we quit or not quit?" Roy opened his eyes, and using a pencil, scribbled, "Not Quit." That was his last communication for two months as he lay in the ICU unit, waging war against the effects of surgery, radiation treatments, and viral and bacterial infections. The machines and medical care kept Roy alive, but his sheer determination saved his life.

> Sometimes quitting is the only way not to quit.

My father was victorious in the fight for his life because he did *not quit*. He was victorious in his remaining four years because he *did quit*. He quit thinking about what he no longer had—good health. He quit comparing himself with what he had been—athletic and vigorous. He quit longing for what he wished were true—that he could do what he had done before and have what was gone. He quit thoughts that focused on the impossible. Sometimes quitting is the only way not to quit.

Roy's problem was a disease; your problem is a person. That's different, or is it? Roy didn't like the disease. You don't like having problems with your screwed-up person (SUP). Roy wanted the disease to stop. You want to have peace in your home, workplace, and community. He sought outside help because the disease was beyond his control. You may need outside help to gain an objective view of your situation. Roy faced a crossroads—continue his struggle to live or give in to death. You must determine whether you are going to live in the tension that now exists, ignore the problems, compromise, or leave—a crossroads. He longed for what he didn't have. You long for what you believe you should have in your relationship. He grieved. You grieve. He chose. You must choose.

Happiness depends on your making an informed choice and accepting the responsibility for that choice. That one step, recognizing who manages your course, is the beginning of learning to be happy—inside, regardless of the outside circumstances. Staying in a relationship—unhappy and bitter—or leaving and clinging to the injustices are both poor course management.

Sometimes the choice about your relationship is made for you by death, divorce, or physical abuse. But you still have a choice: Will you be happy inside, regardless of the outside circumstances? You can be if you find ways to appreciate what you have rather than wishing for what you don't have. Resenting what is or should have been does no one any good. Happiness and success boil down to course management and mental toughness. This means recognizing that every path has its own pluses and minuses.

When Leaving Is Not Optional

It is possible to live victoriously in relationships that are incredibly consuming, limiting, and controlling and still not lose who you are. But sometimes the obstacles are so great and the dysfunction so consuming that to stay in the relationship means the life spirit is sucked from your soul. Some relationships ravish you; they eat you alive, destroy your self-confidence, and riddle you with criticism. They require you to give up your own identity, ideas, ideals, and goals. A relationship out of control, like a disease out of control, is malignant. Sometimes the responsible thing is to leave for the sake of those under your care or for your own mental or physical health. Leaving may be the only positive option when you can no longer survive, when your *self* is dying.

The single most dramatic difference between healthy and toxic relationships is the amount of freedom that exists for each person to express himself or herself as an individual. While healthy relationships encourage individuality, personal responsibility, and independence, unhealthy relationships encourage dependency. Sacrifice and compromise are healthy parts of a relationship. But being required to blindly follow a family member's commands or a supervisor's directives with no opportunity for your own input is toxic. Giving up your needs and aspirations to someone else with whom you are in relationship must be a choice you make based on long-term goals, not the result of the other person exerting his power over you. Losing who you are in the process of serving, helping, giving, or sharing is not only unhealthy, it is toxic. It can happen only when your vision is skewed.

Randy was losing his sense of self. "I've tried to do everything my parents have asked through the years, yet I feel like the bad son. They didn't like my fiancée, so I didn't marry her. For five years I've been the outcast because I moved to North Carolina with my job. I come home all the time, call, do everything I can to appease and please them, but though they never come right out and say it, I feel their hurt. I'm thinking about coming back home."

Randy's choice to relinquish his individuality joined with his parents' unreasonable expectations formed the foundation for a screwed-up relationship. He was on a treadmill, trying to please his parents who controlled him by withdrawing their love. He had allowed his parents' will to become his will.

No one has to leave a relationship to be his own person, but we must stand up in our relationships as adults, without guilt, accepting the responsibility for our choices. Randy left town physically, but he never left emotionally. He still clung to his parents with utter dependency, unwilling to stand as an adult. His problem was not his overprotective parents; it was his own choice to subjugate his will to theirs. Randy needed to get off the fence and manage his course.

Owning Your Choice

I ask six questions of people who are considering whether they are going to quit or not quit their relationship. These questions help them ferret out the possible consequences of their options. I hope you will take the time to sit down with your notebook and answer these questions as honestly as you can. To own your choice, you must discern why the sacrifice you make is worth the effort.

1. What is best for my life long term?
2. What is best long term for those in my care?
3. What *must* I have from this relationship to stay? (Not what you want, would like, or need.)

4. What will I absolutely not tolerate in this relationship if I stay?
5. What am I willing to lose if I end this relationship?
6. What do I expect to gain if I stay in this relationship?

Yes, there are times in all relationships when we may not like each other very much. There are even times when it feels like there is no love left. Emotions are like that. They flatten out occasionally, like a tire with a slow leak. It can be a bumpy experience for everyone on the ride. I imagine that if you are reading this book, you are experiencing a bumpy point in your ride or even a flat-tire time. You may be considering strongly whether the relationship is worth the effort. You must choose, just as Roy did. Your choice requires courage, determination, and commitment—and personal ownership.

Roy's choice affected his entire world. In some ways his quitting would have eased all of us out of a lot of pain. But the choice was his to make. Through the process of hanging tough, he taught his family how to live and how to die with grace. He passed on to his children the sense that if he could make it through such travail with such vigor, so could they. In the long run it was definitely worth our struggle. We all

> The lifeblood of successful living is owning your choices.

sacrificed; we all gained. The difference between our feelings and those of the woman who wrote me about her parents' unhappy relationship was that we knew Roy had made his choice and he owned it. He made the most of his circumstances. He didn't choose and then hang back wishing he had chosen differently.

A counselor once told a woman who was seeking help in keeping her fifteen-year marriage together that her problem was she had given too much. "Next time I'm certainly not going to give all of me!" she exclaimed.

She missed the point. Giving 100 percent is what makes a relationship work, as long as the giving is bounded by respect for each other and for self. The notion that a relationship can exist without compromise and sacrifice is fantasy. The counselor was trying (poorly, I might add) to imply that in her particular case the woman's giving had turned her into a rug. Being walked on in a relationship is unhealthy for everyone—the one being tread on, the ones watching, and the one walking. You cannot have a stable, growing relationship when one of the parties is on the floor licking boots.

I never advise a couple to divorce, a child to leave home, or a parent to give up on a rebellious or dysfunctional kid unless it is evident that verbal or physical abuse has so handicapped the person that she is unable to choose rationally and survival depends on distance from the relationship. Staying in a difficult relationship or ending one should be up to the person who must live with the consequences. If you can't make the relationship work, then look where you have been and design ways to move on to a fulfilling life with other relationships. As much as you would wish it to be different, some relationships are hopeless.

> See what you have—the past; see what you want—the present; and see what can be—the future.

Both staying the course and moving on offer important growth lessons if you are committed to the course you choose. Halfway is not acceptable in building healthy self-esteem. Both choices require that you see what you have—the past; see what you want—the present; and see what can be—the future.

So when should you quit? When is the sacrifice you are making too much to stay?

- Quit when the relationship is so unhealthy that the only way to gain perspective and stay emotionally healthy is distance.
- Quit when there is frequent physical abuse. Physical abusers rarely stop once they have crossed over the line from threats to actual abuse.
- Quit when you are drowning and have no more strength to dog-paddle.
- Quit when someone for whom you are responsible is drowning in verbal or physical abuse and you can take him or her with you.
- Quit if to stay, you must be a doormat.
- Quit if you are willing to own the choice and its consequences.

When should you stay?

- Stay if there is a glimmer of hope to which you can cling.
- Stay if you are the ray of hope for others and, in the staying, *you* will not be destroyed.
- Stay if you are willing to own the choice and its consequences.

The ultimate measure of a man or woman is not where he or she stands in moments of comfort and convenience, but where he or she stands at times of challenge and controversy. Maybe it's time to rethink where you are standing as you attempt to resolve your problems. Your relationship cannot flourish until you get off the fence. It's when you come down, determine your course, and start the journey that your life will begin to change. You can't stand until you find your legs. And you won't be healthy in any relationship if you are not standing on your own.

Settle your commitment to the relationship, one way or the other, knowing that either path exacts a price. Commitment is a decision; it is also a process that gives you back your life. Being passive destroys the possibilities for a healthy relationship, even as it keeps you subservient and feeling victimized. The indispensable first step to getting the things you want out of life is this: Decide what you want.

Lifelines

- Straddling the fence is a death sentence for a relationship.
- The hope is for a new beginning.
- Sometimes quitting is the only way to not quit.
- The lifeblood of successful living is owning your choices.
- See what you have—the past; see what you want— the present; and see what can be—the future.

5

Pull Out the Splinters

*Splinters on our inside find a way to affect our
outside.*

Most relationships and people grow to be screwed up slowly.
As a result it is hard to recognize that the relationship is off
center and out of sync. It seems that arguing, whining, hiding, begging, or avoiding each other are normal. When you
are in such a relationship, you are not surprised to hear of
other relationships that are falling apart—broken marriages,
estranged parents and children, people walking off their jobs,
friendships disintegrating—because you know the weariness
that results from dealing with angry emotions that are often
part of troubled relationships.

Your eyes are open. You are determined to quit straddling
the fence. Even though the person drives you crazy, you are

connected. You intend to stay the course, but you also intend to find ways to stay healthy and be happy. You recognize that spin-offs from your difficult relationship have damaged your other relationships. You are saddened when you think of the time, energy, and emotions that you have spent trying to change someone who does not see a need to change. You are tired of the unhappiness, the guilt, the overwhelming hurt. You say to yourself: *Happiness is my inside job, regardless of the outside circumstances.*

If you are to find contentment in the midst of challenging circumstances, you must get rid of the splinters. Splinters are the wrongs and broken dreams that lie buried within our hearts. Before we can pull out the splinters, there must be a splinter search. That means soul searching, prodding and poking, and it is painful. Many find the hurt too much, the deep inner turmoil too great, the justifications, blame, anger, tears, aching, and longing too arduous to overcome. So they quit, believing that if they ignore the disappointment and hurt festering around the splinter, they will get used to it. The buried splinter, however, continues to produce its poison.

Splinter searches begin with a period of deep inner turmoil and end with a decision: The status quo is no longer acceptable. Reality sets in. You realize that you aren't going to get everything you want from this relationship. If you have needs that aren't met, you will either have to find a way to pick up the slack or let that part of your expectations and dreams go by the wayside. What is no longer acceptable is browbeating your screwed-up person to get him to meet your needs or choose the same goals as you when he is not willing to do so.

This time of splinter searches is the most difficult time in the relationship—harder than the longing times, the sad times, or the angry times. The period feels like you are in a rodeo and your emotions are tossing you in all directions as they bounce off the memories and the unfulfilled dreams. As the memories buck, they bring splinters to the surface. Problems, which were pushed deep inside, rankle.

This is the point when you need to sit yourself down for a pep talk. Tell yourself: I can make it through this turmoil. *This too shall pass, and when it does, I will be a new person, free. The relationship I have will not be the one I fantasize, but the one we develop together. It won't come out of a mold; it will be slowly formed by our choices. What we build will be new. I will use the past as a guide, not my blueprint. This is what a real relationship is all about—finding what works.* The relationship the two of you develop is better than fantasy. It will be earned, nurtured, grown, and uniquely yours.

Reality Fights Expectations

"Mostly it's frustrating. I can't reason with my husband, can't depend on him, can't expect any real support from him, and don't understand why he doesn't understand what I need. Heaven knows, I tell him point-blank. Living with someone is just a lot of work, nothing like I thought it would be! What do you do when your relationship isn't what it is supposed to be?"

> If you want to change your relationship, you must figure out—am I messed up, are you messed up, or are we both doing it wrong?

Ginny's words were a cry for help, no different from those of the teenager who sought advice because she hated her older brother, or the mother-in-law who was vehement about a daughter-in-law's vices. All were focused on what someone was doing wrong that mangled their expectations of the relationship. Each expressed frustration, but as their steam was vented, they began to question, "Is what I feel right or wrong? What if the problem is me?" If you want to change your relationship, you must figure out—am I messed up, are you messed up, or are we both doing it wrong?

Healthy people adjust their fantasies to work with reality.

To a large degree, satisfaction or disappointment in life depends on our putting on glasses to look realistically at what is possible within the relationship so that energy is not wasted waiting and longing for the improbable. Real life is never as perfect as the magical relationships where princes return after fighting their dragons, kiss their beautiful maidens, and change all the bad into good as they move out together toward the sunset. In fantasy, relationship problems always go away. In real life, magic has nothing to do with solving the problems. Hard work is needed to make the necessary *adjustments* and *compromises* as we realize what is possible, what is improbable, and what is simply not going to be. Healthy people adjust their fantasies to work with reality.

Meeting Our Own Needs

People become confused and angry when they figure someone else should fill their needs and it doesn't happen. Ginny's problem wasn't her husband; her problem was her expectations. She believed that her happiness was his responsibility. Relationships with screwed-up people would be hopeless if we expected all of our fulfillment to come from them.

You and I both know that you can understand *why* someone does or doesn't do something and still be driven crazy by his actions. We also recognize that even if someone meets every criteria we have for wonderful, we can still feel like the pits inside. No one can fill *your* needs sufficiently, except *you*.

Each of us is about as happy as we decide to be.

> Each of us is about as happy as we decide to be.

There are no pat answers and easy-to-follow instructions that will fix an unsatisfying relationship. But there are lifelines, guides, that keep you focused and keep you from sinking into frustration and anxiety. It helps to know that an occasional blowup is a normal part of life. Let me caution, however, that if nagging, whining, avoidance, screaming, and put-downs are a constant part of your relationship, this is unhealthy and you should seek ways to change the patterns.

If you are unsure of the reason for the unmet expectations in your relationships, think through the answers to the following questions. These questions will help you pinpoint the problem areas so you can address solutions:

1. Is there something specific we always fight about?
2. What is it I feel is missing?
3. Are we expecting different things from the relationship?
4. Am I helpful or reactive in trying to get to the root of the problem?
5. Is our relationship turmoil within the bounds of healthy or are problem behaviors constant, as mentioned above?
6. Are there ways to fill my needs without compromising my relationship?
7. What can I do to make myself happy where I am?

Coming to grips with the reality that happiness is an inside decision that is determined by the conscious choice to make the best of what you have will help you stop blaming others and start plugging in the holes and pulling out the splinters so that you can know real contentment. Don't give up.

Finding Outside Support

Seeking fulfillment outside the relationship is sometimes the only way you can survive with a screwed-up person. Be sure that the outside support comes from a healthy source. For example, escaping through drugs or alcohol is not a healthy option. The list of healthy possibilities for finding fulfillment is as varied as the individuals who need it. Consider these options:

- Get involved in a new hobby.
- Enroll in a course.
- Do volunteer work.
- Start an exercise program.
- Schedule a time for your favorite form of relaxation—reading, walking in the park, visiting a museum, going to a movie.
- Plan special times—trips, dinner parties, holiday celebrations.
- Give a helping hand to someone in need.
- Make an effort to get to know your neighbors.
- Develop new friendships.
- Express thanks to others through phone calls and notes.

The difference between the words *victor* and *victim* are two little letters. The difference between mere survival and successful living in a difficult relationship may be adjust-

Difficult relationships offer lessons in what to do and what not to do.

ing to what is possible, rather than wishing for what is unlikely to be. Difficult relationships, in many ways, are a great blessing, rather than the worst thing in life. They offer lessons in what to do and what not to do, even as they offer an opportunity to build a unique creation from the ingredients at hand.

Relationships are not like ships. They can rise again, even when all seems lost. Hang in there. Don't let a good thing die. If your expectations are part of the problem, causing your relationship with your SUP to skew, it's time to make some adjustments. Get rid of the splinters. Change your focus, your attitude, and your expectations, and you may find that things improve considerably.

Lifelines

- If you want to change your relationship, you must figure out—am I messed up, are you messed up, or are we both doing it wrong?
- Healthy people adjust their fantasies to work with reality.
- Each of us is about as happy as we decide to be.
- Difficult relationships offer lessons in what to do and what not to do.

6

Heal the Hidden Wound

No one will improve your lot if you do not.

Remember the old saying, "Sticks and stones may break my bones, but words can never hurt me"? It's not true. When people relate to each other by hurling insulting names, belittling criticism, and degrading comments, internal bleeding begins. When they hide hurtful acts behind loving words, bruises form. When they say, "You never do it right! You don't measure up! You aren't what I expected. You are such a failure," the twinkle inside us dies. Broken bones heal more easily than a spirit that is wounded by abusive words or acts. A battered

> Broken bones heal more easily than a spirit that is wounded by abusive words or acts.

and broken spirit limps through life seeking affirmation, or strikes out to prove "I'm okay," by being bigger and better.

The way we feel about ourselves and the way we treat others or allow others to treat us depend on what we have learned from our childhood experiences. If you live with encouragement, you learn to be confident. If you live with praise, you encourage others. If you live with approval, you want to affirm. If you live with recognition, you reach toward goals. If you live with generosity, you learn to share. If you live with honesty and fairness, you know what truth and justice are. If you live with security, you have faith in yourself and in those around you. If you live with friendliness, you learn that the world is a nice place in which to live.[1]

If, on the other hand, you live with the opposites— disapproval, ridicule, criticism, rejection, put-downs, selfishness, lies, injustice, cruelty, and harshness, you withdraw into fears, seek approval through treadmills of performance, feel like a failure or that approval is only temporary regardless of your performance, reject faith or flaunt it, or grow greedy, bitter, commanding, controlling, and/or disillusioned.

Disintegration in Relationships

Recognizing how our past affects our present is crucial, especially in light of the natural tendency of everything in the universe to move from order to disorder. The principle that governs this drift is called the law of disintegration. Engineers and scientists sometimes call it the law of entropy. The universe is expanding outward. The sun and all the stars are slowly burning themselves out. All man-made materials that fill the landfills are becoming compost. Your car is deteriorating from the day you drive it home from the showroom. Your body is slowly aging and dying. James Dobson notes that, not so surprisingly, human relationships also conform to this principle. They drift away from each other unless there is an intentional effort to pull together. Disintegration is the natural order; cohesion is a choice.

Abuse is disintegration in progress. Like a disease, abuse infects the victim and spreads out to affect others. Victims of

> **Disintegration is the natural order; cohesion is a choice.**

abuse grow to believe the abuse is an acceptable, normal interchange between people. Only early in the game, or as a result of outside intervention by family or friends, can most abuse victims separate reality from the misconceptions that have developed through the years of unhealthy exchanges.

Becoming Used to Abuse

We will be less confused about what constitutes abusive behavior if we keep in mind that words or acts can do to the spirit what a vacuum cleaner does to dirt—suck you in and entrap you. That is abuse. Abuse is often couched in "I care" missiles that leave their victims at a loss to know *who* is the problem. The words or acts cut to the core. We have all felt the sting of words that catch us by surprise with an unexpected insult or piercing rejection. When such debasing actions are the foundation of a relationship, abuse reigns. The behavior causes the target of abuse to feel off-balance, inferior, incapable, irresponsible, clumsy, undeserving, and unlovable. Tension and friction reign.

It may be unclear exactly where the line is between caring that corrects and caring that mutilates the spirit, between controlling for safety and healthy development and psychological abuse. Yet for the sake of those you care about, for your sake, for the sake of someone who abuses, if there are signs that the behavior is skewing, help is needed immediately. The three markers of abusive behavior are belittlement, manipulation, and control.

Caring, or love, crosses the line to abuse when it consistently exhibits any of the following characteristics:

- excessive overprotection
- given with strings
- withdrawing or withholding love or appreciation
- physical or emotional violence
- acceptance based on performance

Abuse can cloud reality. It may be perceived to be normal and acceptable if you have grown up with it. If you seem to be the only target, you may wonder: *Am I too sensitive? Am I doing something wrong?* If no one else seems to see the problem, you ask, *Am I making too big a deal out of this?* If everyone but you seems to think the person is wonderful, you think, *What's wrong with me?* If the abuse is couched in "for your own good" but it doesn't feel good, you question your judgment. Did I cause the problem? Should I apologize? Am I bad? How can I do better?

> The three markers of abusive behavior: belittlement, manipulation, and control.

Abuse may be difficult to identify because of the packaging. It may sound like: I am only saying this because I care so much . . . You made me yell at you . . . I know I shouldn't say this, but . . . You can't understand like I do . . . I just tell it like it is . . . You shouldn't take it so personally . . . I feel responsible to set you straight . . . I said no! The issue is not up for discussion . . . You can't begin to appreciate how much I sacrifice for you.

Through the years I have wept for those who questioned their own value because someone they needed—a spouse, parent, sibling, relative, friend, boss—treated them like an old shoe to be stepped on and tossed aside. It takes a good friend, an outsider, some caring individual to help a person who has been beaten down stand as an adult.

These are a few statements I've heard that echoed loudly the mistreatment, while the victim flogged herself for causing the problem.

> "I wished that he would beat me. I thought that if I could see a broken limb, a bloody lip, a bruise, I would know that what was happening to me was real—not just in my head."

> "I shouldn't be such a wimp. The boss is always right."

> "I remember feeling like all I wanted to do was jump out and kill myself after he screamed incessantly in the car for over an hour, pounding the steering wheel, gesturing, and threatening."

> "Once my father left me and my son in the parking lot in a strange town because my son was tired and had been fussy in the car. He couldn't stand the noise anymore."

> "My mom did her best, but I was a bad kid."

Be careful if you find yourself apologizing for everything you do, allowing people to constantly put you down, always feeling compelled to lead your life according to what another thinks, believing you are the cause for someone else's wrong behavior, feeling the need to sneak around, or feeling that no one takes your ideas or suggestions seriously. Your self-esteem is limping.

Reactions to Abuse

Rarely do we correct or defend ourselves against subtle abuse. We may not recognize it as abuse. We may be trying to be polite—nice, respectful of authority, not overreacting, trying to see it from the other person's perspective. We may fear that any response on our part will bring a storm of anger or a host of manipulative reactions. We may question our own feelings. We may be caught off guard and find it difficult to discern whether the comment or action was truly meant the way we perceived it.

We should be appalled by statements such as these that leave the described individual on the defensive: You aren't going to have another helping, are you, fatty? . . . Sweetheart, when are you going to grow up and act your age? . . . Meet my son. He's as mean as a snake in the grass. . . . My old woman isn't much to look at, but can she cook! . . . Son, you aren't nearly the athlete your brother is. . . . My husband is such a slob.

Abusive interactions cause you to:

- hide your true feelings
- avoid the difficult person—and others
- sneak around
- criticize
- explode with anger
- put yourself down
- apologize
- fear disapproval

- simmer
- expect the worst
- believe your perfect performance is the key to acceptance
- feel an excessive need for privacy

Abusive behavior doesn't just go away. It grows in the shadows as the victim's self-esteem weakens and the abuser becomes more captive to his own pernicious behaviors. To stop this cycle, abuse must be recognized as wrong. It does not matter how often it happens—abuse is wrong. It doesn't matter if it targets only one individual—it is wrong. Whether it takes place in the family or the workplace, it is wrong. Keep in mind that allowing yourself to be abused repeatedly will cause you to lose your *self*. If a spouse is abusing you, this behavior has the potential to set horrific patterns into the lives of your children, who may grow up to allow or inflict similar abuse.

> Cruel words do to the spirit what a vacuum cleaner does to dirt—suck you in and entrap you.

An indication that hurtful behavior is abusive is its frequency. A young woman in her second marriage talked about her mother-in-law problems. The in-law saw her as an outlaw. She ignored, ridiculed, and left her out. She brought gifts to her son's children by his first wife but did not bring anything to her grandson by this second wife. She justified this by saying, "He has too many toys. I don't need to add to his pile." She challenged her daughter-in-law's decisions. And when the young woman tried to open the door of communication between them a crack by asking her to share her secrets of raising beautiful roses, she laughed, "Forget it, honey. You would never have the stick-to-it ability that raising roses requires."

I asked this stressed-out young woman if her mother-in-law was always so brutal.

"Always!" she said emphatically.

"Aren't you lucky!" I replied. "Your mother-in-law's hurtful behavior can be counted on, so you recognize she is the one with a problem, not you."

As an adult the young woman needs and should expect respect, even as she is respectful. It is not all right for someone to be cruel. And it is doubly wrong for adults to allow this action to affect the children in their care.

Healthy adults set limits to the guff they will take. Pledge to yourself, out loud, repeatedly, until you begin to act, "As an adult (age is irrelevant), I am responsible to:

- refuse to see myself through the eyes of someone who only sees my failures
- act responsibly, not blaming my actions on others
- express my real needs and feelings
- compromise and negotiate fairly
- respect others and expect respect
- find my own interests
- set limits and boundaries
- face the truth
- carry out my responsibilities and commitments from a base of love, not merely obligation

Check Your Discernment

We are responsible for what we do and what we allow. Allowing degrading treatment causes reactive, defensive behavior, which spins off to hurt everyone. I often ask people who feel manipulated and controlled to visualize themselves as a top. Then I ask, "Who starts you spinning?" Once you visualize who starts you spinning, you can visualize stopping it. No one can spin someone who refuses to respond. Spinning happens because we won't face the reality. Test your discernment. The following five scenarios cover many of the boundary and limit issues in normal, daily life. Choose the option that most closely follows what you would do if confronted with a similar situation. At the end of the exercise, see how many "healthy" answers you gave. Your honest choices can affirm your ability to set healthy limits and boundaries or point out that your discernment and boundaries are blurred.

Scenario 1

Bill's parents invited his family to come for Christmas Day dinner at 11:00 A.M. Late is not acceptable. Bill's family wants to visit, but the timing will cause a lot of stress and spoil their own family time. Santa doesn't even arrive until Christmas morning.

> *Choice A:* Go anyway at the set time. Bill's parents are old and set in their ways. They won't be around many more years.
>
> *Choice B:* Be gracious, but state a reasonable time for your family to arrive. If this is not acceptable, stay home, enjoy your own family, and perhaps invite Bill's parents to come to your home for dessert or set another date to get together.

Scenario 2

There's a knock on Pam's door. It's the boss with work that he forgot to ask her to do at the office. He has a letter he would like to get out in the evening mail. Pam has evening plans.

> *Choice A:* Drop the plans. The boss comes first.
>
> *Choice B:* Say that you are sorry but you have plans. Offer to do the letter first thing in the morning when you come to work.

Scenario 3

Your daughter has called to ask you to babysit for the third time this week. It's not a crisis or crucial but, of course, important to her. If you babysit, you must cancel important, though not crucial, plans of your own.

> *Choice A:* Help her. After all, these are your grandchildren and it isn't easy being a young mother.
>
> *Choice B:* Say, "I already have plans, but please call me next time. Whenever I am free I love to have the children visit."

Scenario 4

Your doorbell rings. It is a neighbor who is going through a major life crisis. She comes almost every day and stays for hours. You want to help, for you know people are more important than schedules, but you have other responsibilities that demand your attention.

> *Choice A:* Stop what you're doing. How can you tell her you don't have time for her?
>
> *Choice B:* Explain that you have commitments already for the day. Suggest another time to get together.

Scenario 5

Your husband calls and says he must stay at work so he won't be home in time to watch the children so you can go to your meeting.

Choice A: Pout. Stay home feeling the unfairness of life and inconsideration of your husband.

Choice B: Find alternative child care and don't stew about the cost. If an alternative is not available, accept the reality that your children come first. If this is a consistent pattern, plan on alternatives.

Option *B* is the best choice in each scenario. The more *A* choices you made, the more confused your boundaries and limits have become and the more likely you are to be feeling used and abused. People spin because they expect problems to resolve themselves. Quit expecting a magical solution. Magic does not solve problems or heal hidden wounds. Good, proactive choices do.

> People spin because they expect problems to resolve themselves.

Am I Okay? Are You Okay?

In the seventies Thomas Harris wrote a book that became a bestseller titled *I'm OK—You're OK* in which he described the four major relationship positions.[2] I have created a chart that defines the four relationships and provides an exercise that can help you visualize your particular relationship. Only the fourth position provides a solid foundation for healthy adult interactions.

Relationship Positions

Self-Esteem	Position	Symbolizes	Health of the Relationship
1. I'm okay; you're not okay.	Place one hand representing you on top of the other.	Superiority	Skewed
2. You're okay; I'm not okay.	Place hand representing you under other hand.	Inferiority	Skewed
3. Neither of us is okay.	Place both hands in air.	Both feel inferiority.	Skewed
4. I'm okay; you're okay.	Place hands side by side.	Both have healthy self-esteem.	Healthy

How Abusers See Themselves

Abusers don't see themselves as bad guys. They justify their abuse—I'm helping. . . . I care. . . . It's my responsibility. Even Al Capone, the notorious gangster boss who during Prohibition in the Roaring Twenties in Chicago tortured and killed his enemies without mercy, wondered why people thought he was a bad person. "Why would anyone think of me as the bad guy? I was only giving them what they wanted [alcohol]." How much more unlikely it is for someone who hasn't murdered, broken laws, or lived an immoral life to feel like a culprit.

Perhaps you are the abuser. Have you skewed from healthy interactions to unhealthy? Read through the following checklist. If even one applies to the way you relate to someone, *you* may be the problem. Get professional help if your relationships seem to sour, you constantly experience friction, and you have checked several of these abusive behaviors. It is never too late to change negative behaviors, but often it takes an objective outsider to help us recognize destructive habits and unhealthy patterning.

Abusive people:

- constantly correct others
- put others down for doing things differently than they would do them
- use jokes or critical remarks to ridicule
- correct people publicly
- think their ideals and beliefs are gospel
- believe they are innately superior
- justify hurtful actions by saying, "That's just the way I am!"
- disregard the feelings of others
- justify severe punishment

Take Charge

If someone is victimizing you with any abusive behavior, your relationship has skewed and your self-esteem is diminished. Self-talk is crucial to jump-start battered confidence. Tell yourself: I can change what I think of myself and how I interact in this relationship. Encourage yourself to take the necessary steps, regardless of what anyone else does. Gather your ever-diminishing inner resources to identify the problem and seek outside help, separate from the other person until you are healthy enough to cope, or do both if you have crossed from a skewed relationship to a screwed-up relationship. Take courage in the fact that first steps are the beginning of change. Don't be discouraged by the effort required, time

> The first step toward healing hidden wounds is the recognition that there is a problem that must be resolved.

needed, or setbacks you experience. Change takes time. Be patient with yourself and you will gradually regain self-confidence and be able to say no to the abuse.

Know When to Stop

In the movie *War Games*, a U.S. government computer was programmed to start a global nuclear war. Once the program was set in motion, all attempts to alter it were futile. At the last second the computer stopped itself, saying: "Interesting game. The only way to win is not to play." The only way to win in a relationship that is entangled by abuse is to stop playing the game.

Lifelines

- Broken bones heal more easily than a spirit that is wounded by abusive words or acts.
- Disintegration is the natural order; cohesion is a choice.
- Cruel words do to the spirit what a vacuum cleaner does to dirt—suck you in and entrap you.
- Tell yourself you are at a new beginning.
- The first step toward healing hidden wounds is the recognition that there is a problem that must be resolved.
- People spin because they expect problems to resolve themselves.

7

Can Ailing Relationships
Make You Sick?

*Getting out of the swamp depends on your
willingness to step through the mire.*

"I'm sick," Marie said, coughing into a Kleenex. "I've been
sick since I was fourteen. I don't have time to make friends.
I feel like I am in a circle going nowhere with people around
me who just make it worse."

Can your family, close friends, or those with whom you
work and play make you sick? Absolutely. Why? Simply put,
we are bonded to them emotionally, spiritually, physically, and
chemically. Statements such as, You make me sick . . . make
me want to vomit . . . drive me crazy . . . break my heart . . .
are a pain in the neck, imply the reality: People can literally
make you sick or keep you healthy.

Think back to the last time you felt upset, uptight, frustrated, depressed, guilty, or angry. You may have been stuck in traffic, worried about your job, or wishing you could play golf instead of mow the lawn. But based on my experience, I suspect that when those emotions are the strongest, they are ignited by other people, probably your spouse, child, parent, friend, neighbor, or coworker. We are social creatures, and what others do affects us. It affects our emotions, and emotions are drivers of our health.

So should we avoid people who cause our blood pressure to rise? Socrates would say yes! Centuries ago he, like his contemporary Hippocrates, taught that the body could not be cured without concern for the mind—what we think is what we are or will become, and thoughts are definitely influenced by those around us. Today Norman Cousins, in *Anatomy of an Illness,* points out the debilitating influence of negativity on recovery from many critical illnesses, in contrast to the rehabilitating influence of laughter and encouragement.[1] Dr. Bernie Siegel asks people who come to him for medical treatment, "Why did you need this disease?" His comment might stretch the point, but there is no question that there is a strong correlation between our emotional health and our physical health.[2]

Research shows that malfunctioning relationships and relationship breakup put people at much higher risk for both psychiatric and physical disease—even cancer. In 1974 in Alameda County, California, Dr. Lisa Berkman found in a study of 7,000 people that those who had positive social ties had a death rate two to three times lower than those who were isolated. The ten-year University of Michigan study of 2,754 adults in Tecumseh, Michigan, echoed these findings. People with satisfying social contacts had one-quarter the mortality rate of those without supportive networks.[3]

Dr. David Larson, a research psychiatrist for a dozen years with the federal government and now president of the National Institute of Healthcare Research, said, "How we feel affects our health. For instance, being divorced and a nonsmoker is only slightly less dangerous than smoking a pack or more of cigarettes a day and staying married. Every type of terminal cancer strikes divorced individuals of either sex, both white and non-white, more frequently than it does married people."[4] J. J. Lynch, author of *The Broken Heart: The Medical Consequences of Loneliness,* reveals that single men are twice as likely to die from heart disease, stroke, hypertension, and cancer as married men in any given year! And death for the divorced is four times more likely via auto accidents and suicide, seven times higher from cirrhosis of the liver and pneumonia, and eight times greater from murder. Psychiatric illness is ten times more likely.[5]

> Our health is tied to our emotions; emotions are tied to relationships.

Similarly, Larson cites a study of twenty thousand white women between the ages of eighteen and fifty-five that found married women far less prone to physical illness than single women, who suffer more chronic conditions and spent more days in bed than did the married women. A divorced woman's odds of dying in a given year from cancer of the mouth, digestive organs, lungs, and breast are two to three times that of a married woman.[6] Our health is tied to our emotions; emotions are tied to relationships.

Are Emotions Drivers of Physical Health?

The mind controls the body through the release or withholding of morphinelike hormone substances such as serotonin.

These morphinelike substances trigger neuron transmitters to chemically jump-start the electrical messages that transfer from neuron to neuron. The neurotransmitter fibers that carry the electrical message do not touch the neurons and so are dependent on the chemicals to stimulate the electrical transfer, almost as if a plug lying one inch from the electrical outlet is dependent on someone putting it into the outlet for the transfer of electricity to occur. The morphinelike substances create energy like a spark plug to fire the transmission between the neurons.

The marvel of these chemicals is that what we do or think affects their release. For instance, exercise will stimulate the hormones and produce a "runner's high," a sense of well-being. Likewise, positive emotions stimulate the production of these hormones, keeping us balanced and feeling good. Good reinforces good.

The morphinelike substances also react instantly to such drivers as fear and anxiety, producing adrenaline, which causes the body to tense into a protective mode for "fight and flight." In times of high tension the same substances, by slowing their production, cause us to be numb. This slows thinking, reaction time, memory, and decision making. In addition, we may feel tongue-tied and tired and experience numbed emotions. This slowing of the transfer allows time for our mental processes to evaluate the problem that is causing the stress and work proactively, rather than reactively through adrenaline-driven responses.

Studies at Duke University indicate that stress also affects the rate at which our bodies heal. Cell tissue actually heals faster when we are under little stress, as opposed to situations of high stress such as those stimulated by fear. This is confirmed by studies at the University of Washington School of Medicine research department, which concludes that 75 percent of all ill health and healing is affected by the body's reaction to stress.[7]

You recognize the power of emotions to wash you with invigorating energy as a sudden rush of adrenaline increases the heart and respiration rates when you have been surprised or frightened. You know the warm, fuzzy feelings stimulated by friendship and the all-consuming high of new love. You have experienced the down, blue feelings that come in difficult times. Emotions have power to affect how you feel. So how do you feel in relationships that cause high levels of stress? You feel tired, exhausted, volcanic, numbed, and, perhaps, ill. As stress causes the slowing of production of the morphinelike substances, the ability to think clearly, the motivation to change, or the stamina to handle life with enthusiasm are all depleted. The slowed production of the hormones negatively affects T-cell production, which, in turn, affects the immune system capability.

Being sick may start in the emotions, but it ends in the body. Research is showing an increasing appreciation for the reality that your health is in your hands. You must develop healthy coping skills or your emotions will become toxic. Studies confirm that two years after an intense period of stress, for example, the death of a spouse or child, major health problems such as cancers and strokes are common. The Holmes-Rahe Life Events Test assigns numerical values to correlate with the amount of internal stress the body typically experiences in major life events: Death of a spouse is assigned 100 points, divorce 73, separation 65, death of a close family friend 63, a serious relationship conflict 45. Even positive events are stressful: having a baby 39, graduating from college 26.[8]

Stress is inevitable and even good to a point. But in negative relationships that keep us in stewing tensions, as in major

What begins in
the head ends up
affecting the body.

negative life crises, the sooner we get our emotions in check, the less likely we are to damage our health. Allowing negative emotions to simmer and then boil is comparable to slowly dripping water into your computer. It takes time to recognize the harm, but the small drips over time will short-circuit the system. Likewise, the tension drips that begin in our head will end up negatively affecting our body.

Controlling the Control Center

Knowing what helps ease the tension and stimulate the production of hormones that give us a feeling of well-being is crucial as we handle the up-and-down emotions that swirl around screwed-up people. You can't stop negative thoughts and the resulting emotions when you are coping in difficult situations with people who are hard to get along with, but you can keep those feelings from overwhelming you by controlling what you allow to play over and over in your mind.

To stop negative
thoughts, lift the
needle on your mental
record player.

It's all right to be angry, hurt, sad, concerned, confused, and bewildered as long as you don't stay stuck in those emotions. A woman in a seminar shared with the group the secret of her control: "I learned to pick the needle up on my record player." Like all of us, she couldn't stop the thoughts from coming, but she could stop them from playing over and over in her mind.

You may be thinking, *I can't help how I feel. If you had to deal with the boss [or whomever] I have, the buckshot in your rear would drive your emotions helter-skelter too.* I can't change how I feel because I can't leave my husband . . . give up on my kid . . . kick out my father . . . It's impossible to walk away or ignore the creep.

It's true. You can't just ignore or walk away from many of the people with whom you may seriously disagree or with whom it is impossible to live or work amicably. Yet no one controls your thoughts, except you. Stop clinging to the wrong the other person does. Move on mentally. Say loudly and clearly, "I am in charge of me." Good health depends on your control of your mind. The following suggestions may help you get a handle on your thoughts.

The "Do" List of Mind Control

1. **Exercise.** Exercise increases the hormone substances that stimulate the neurotransmitters, thus increasing well-being, lowering stress, and keeping the mind alert.
2. **Praise yourself.** Encouragement is crucial to well-being when handling irregular behavior.
3. **Make guilt productive.** Healthy guilt is a tool, not a weapon; a lesson, not a flogging.
4. **Discern.** Recognizing who owns the wrong behavior frees you from unnecessary anguish.
5. **Find a friend or mentor.** Objective listeners can shine light into the darkness.
6. **Determine your course.** Journeys go nowhere without direction.
7. **Keep a diary of progress.** Write down sunshine happenings.
8. **Accept responsibility for you—and your health.**

Physical exercise, positive thoughts, and firm decisions that keep you from straddling the fence concerning your relationship ease emotional tension and actually produce a high. Perhaps you have experienced such a high after commitment to a decision following a period of wavering and indecision. You may feel this high after determin-

> Being physically sick can be caused by being mentally stressed.

ing your relationship direction. You will be energized and feel a sense of well-being. Maintaining that enthusiasm and spark after the initial burst of adrenaline depends on clear-sighted realism that recognizes change is an inside decision that is affirmed by small gains, as well as major moves.

Encourage Yourself and Others

When rescue workers approach an accident victim, their first task is encouragement: "You are going to be all right. You are hurt, but we are here to help. You can make it. You are going to be safe." They know the power the mind has to control shock, so they attempt to focus the victim on the positives, the possibilities, as opposed to the horrors and danger. You may not be facing the problems of an accident, but the same advice applies to relationship problems: Hang tight. Don't succumb. Keep your fear and anger under control. Reach out for help. You can overcome.

I wish we were sitting together sharing our thoughts. I would ask you several questions that have helped me think seriously about the connection between my health and my relationships. Let me just list them. You may save yourself from a multitude of health problems brought on by negative thoughts if you can recognize *who causes your tension* (the other guy) and *who is responsible for developing healthy ways to cope with the stress* (you).

1. Think about a time you remember being bathed in happy emotions. How did you feel? How long did those feelings last?
2. Think about a time you remember being uptight and upset. How did you feel? How long did it take you to rebalance and calm your emotions?

3. Is there someone with whom you deal who causes your emotions to skew? How do you feel after being with him or her?
4. If you had to choose someone to spend a day with, who would it be? How do you feel after being with that person?

Did the questions help you focus on the way someone in particular affects your emotions? Are you pinpointing someone who has become the focus of your negative, swirling emotions? Your health, your wholeness, your emotional stability, your happiness depend on whether you control—or allow someone else's behavior to control—what you think. Be kind to yourself. Encourage yourself—and those you reach out to help. Wrap yourself in patience and remember that every family and most work places have a few eccentrics, and that's what makes it challenging—and special.

Lifelines

- Our health is tied to our emotions; emotions are tied to relationships.
- What begins in the head ends up affecting the body.
- To stop negative thoughts, lift the needle on your mental record player.
- Being physically sick can be caused by being mentally stressed.

8

Handling Frazzled Emotions

As long as the eyes leak, the head won't swell.

If you want to live successfully with screwed-up people, you must control the chaos that swirls off your interaction. A person who drives you nuts twists your emotions into stewing turmoil as her actions negatively affect and threaten your needs, financial security, family, friendships, job, reputation, and dreams. A difficult person holds a lot of power—or at least it feels like it—over your life. Perhaps the person who sends your emotions plummeting is your wife. If you leave her, you lose your children. Perhaps it is a parent who will align the whole family against you if you go against his will. Maybe you struggle against a boss who whittles to your core and then pushes you to do things you know are destructive, hurtful, and wrong, but you need the job. If you speak your mind, share your thoughts, or counter her direction, it may cause you to lose something you hold dear.

Even though you want to believe being good enough, giving enough, or being overpowering enough will turn the frog into a prince, it is not going to happen unless a miracle comes from above! Screwed-up people are messed up. Something is wrong with their wiring. You aren't going to change a malfunctioning unit just because you want her to change, regardless of how out of control you become. So what do you do? Is your only choice to live with the situation and stuff the emotions? Stuffing is bad for the psyche. Stuffed emotions simmer; they don't go away.

The situation feels impossible when your emotions are frayed and vulnerable. You feel like you are being hit by a whirling dervish of feelings that cut and flatten you like a pancake. You believe your SUP holds a godlike power over your life. Get hold of yourself. If you are being held by the throat by irregular tactics today, you will feel strangled in the future. You must make a conscious decision to stop trying to change her and start changing your interaction with her. Not only do you stand to lose what you are so fearful of losing if the relationship does not change, but more important, you stand to lose *you*!

Face Reality

The unresolvable issues with a difficult person keep your emotions in a pressure cooker—hot, steaming, under a lot of pressure, and explosive. Overcoming their power depends on your making a determination to use the force of your will to control your feelings. You may never receive appre-

ciation, love, and respect from this individual, but still you
are responsible:

- for your actions and responses
- to carry out your duties to the best of your abilities
- to maintain the highest ethics, regardless of pressure
  to lower the bar
- to act with maturity, regardless of the immaturity of
  anyone around you
- for your attitude
- for compromising when possible to keep a healthy balance within the relationship
- to support and encourage, regardless of whether you
  are supported and encouraged
- for changing the way you respond if your responses to
  an irregular person are born out of anger, as opposed
  to sorrow for the joys they miss by their controlling and
  demeaning attitudes.

Emotions are neither good nor bad. Emotions simply are.
What is bad is the way a skewed relationship affects the delicate balance in which emotions coexist with reason. Reason
must guide the emotions, like a parent with a potentially
unruly child. It is not that the child is bad, but when he
becomes overactive, his behavior can be destructive. Reason
provides discipline for the emotions as it turns overactivity
into creativity.

It may help you understand this concept if you think of a
circle. Emotions and reason exist as partners in a circle that
under normal conditions is about equally divided between
the two. Injustice, unfairness, and unreasonableness skew
that balance as emotions frantically fight for control. They
scramble and push reason to a tiny space in the outermost

part of the circle. Emotions become more and more active until they are frenetic. Reason keeps trying to intercede, to calm the increasing panic or rage. But reason's efforts are like trying to put air back into a burst balloon. It may succeed momentarily until a wave of emotion breaks through, pushing reason aside to wash you in rage, panic, or despair.

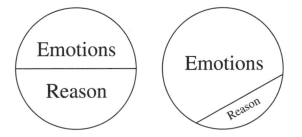

"That's the time for a good cigarette break—or a stiff drink," Jake commented. "I feel the anger filling every part of me so that I could easily go and lambaste my boss. I have to get away until I can get my anger under control." Jake was in a typical out-of-control relationship, feeling helpless to change its power over his life. He did need a break, but there are more positive ways of handling the intensity of these emotions. We will discuss them a little later.

The frayed emotions are activated by triggers from a past indiscretion, a current problem, a long-ago hurt, or a major injustice. These emotions may hang on the shirttail of the current emotions and bolster their intensity when conflict arises. They popcorn, hitting you again and again, from every direction. To reset the balance, reason must force the emotions back into proper proportion.

Overcoming the control of emotions is like trying to handle a huge watermelon in your apartment-sized refrigerator. With the watermelon in the refrigerator, nothing else will fit. To be rid of the watermelon, you must eat it. Eat too fast and your stomach cramps. Eat too slowly and the watermelon rots. It's the same with raging, unpredictable emotions. They are too big to handle all at once. If they are left to their own devices, however, they take over, leaving little room for positive emotions to exist. It is not hard to recognize when the positive emotions are struggling. That's when laughter leaves.

Appreciate Your Emotions

Many of us believe that having negative emotions is bad. We tell ourselves that if we aren't happy in a relationship, there is something wrong with it. Perhaps that's true. Emotions are to be respected, appreciated, and accepted for what they are—signals that alert us to the way we perceive our experiences. They are tools that apprise us of how we feel toward the actions of others just as a thermometer gauges the outside temperature. At the same time, we must remember that emotions are childlike. They play. They tire. And when they are tired, they don't feel good. When you are feeling down about your relationships, when the interchanges get to you, rest. Take a break. Do something different, interesting, and enjoyable.

Healthy emotions develop from listening to the affirmations and the alarms of your feelings. When someone treats you disrespectfully, recognize the pain. It's the same as when someone steps on your foot; it hurts. Healthy people acknowledge the pain; they know stepping on someone is wrong. Accepting that a hurtful action is wrong gives you a handle for dealing with it, a way to let it go, to be a bigger person, to feel sorrow for the smallness of someone else.

Work *with* your emotions, as opposed to *for* your emotions. When emotions are given free rein, they:

- are nearsighted and childish
- demand our attention
- make us think only feelings count
- convince us that life is not fair
- decry injustice
- support pity parties
- point fingers at others
- defend our actions, right or wrong
- want instant gratification
- make us self-centered—*my* needs, *my* wants, *my* feelings

Reason encourages emotions to slow down when they begin to become overbearing. Reason talks realistically to you about the trade-off of long-term happiness for feel-good now. Your emotions, on the other hand, plead for instant gratification, even if it will be harmful in the long term. Reason points out that life never has been fair—so what? Reason asks: Is your plan to deal with that reality going to resolve the problem or just make it worse? Reason points out that feelings can paralyze unless you make the concerted effort to harness their power. We'll discuss how to do that later in this chapter.

> When someone steps on your foot, it hurts.

Out-of-Control Feelings

Be aware that emotions that control you paralyze you. Six distinct feelings vie for the controls when you are struggling to keep balance in difficult relationships. As we look at each one of these feelings briefly, try to reflect how many times you use one of these feelings as an excuse for not going, not doing, not standing as an adult in your difficult relationship.

I Can't!

I can't sounds like, I would if I could, but I just can't. With reason, *I can't* changes to *I can*. Tremendous empowerment flows from recognizing you really can handle the challenges of your relationship. Say out loud, "I can stand up. I can set limits and boundaries. I can be an adult."

I'm Alone!

I'm alone sounds like, No one has ever had such a problem as this. Reason points out that no one is alone. Many people have similar relationship problems, and overcoming the challenge will equip you to help others who will look to you as their guide.

I'm Different!

I'm different sounds like, No one will like me because I'm not like anyone else. Freedom is born when reason makes you aware of your uniqueness, as well as how you are like others. One of the ways we are alike is that everyone has challenges to overcome in relationships.

I'm Going Crazy!

I'm going crazy sounds like, I can't remember, can't sleep, can't think straight. Reason helps you appreciate that lethargy dulls the pain of hurting relationships and that thinking straight is possible, even though it seems elusive.

I'm Hurting!

I'm hurting sounds like, I can't believe he did this to me! Rejection, unfairness, and broken commitments hurt. However, linked with reason, these terrible feelings teach the critical value of being fair, just, true, and loving without reserve. Suffering, linked with reason, builds empathy for the plight of others and appreciation for one's own ability to overcome.

I'm Guilty!

I'm guilty sounds like, What could I have done differently? Reason uses guilt to point out

> Progress flows from working with your emotions, as opposed to for your emotions.

your responsibility for an action and change. This may be the most constructive of all emotions because it focuses you on the reality that you are responsible for what you do. You are responsible for you.

Analyze the Problem

When you are in a difficult relationship, you won't have much energy for analysis, but be aware that if you are making such statements as the following, your emotions are probably in the driver's seat. Get help.

- I would call for help, but I can't.
- I would reach out to others, but I can't.
- I feel so alone.
- I don't know what to do or what to say.
- If I go left, I should have gone right.
- If I do what I think will help, it may create harm.

- Even when I try to stay calm, I get so angry and out of control that I lose it.
- If you had a screwed-up person in your life, like mine, you would be nuts too.
- Nothing I do works.
- I didn't start this.
- I just wish he would die.
- I want her to change, then I would be all right.

Harness the Power

When you stew in your emotions, you're like an egg in hot water. You may look the same on the outside, but the longer you simmer, the harder you become on the inside. Grudges, depression, anguish, obsession, and bitterness are harbored under your shell and show in your eyes and attitude.

Here's what happens to your emotions as you deal within difficult relationships if you do not free yourself from their stranglehold:

Love becomes a sick obsession.

Anger turns into rage.

The need for affirmation becomes a drive.

Caring is given only to receive something in return.

Sadness becomes anguish.

Grief becomes wretchedness.

Happiness becomes a driven addiction to find fulfillment.

Finding ways to handle the negative feelings requires conscious thought on your part. In chapter 17, counseling helps are discussed. Talking to an outsider who can lend objective insights without feeling the need to direct your steps is beneficial. Exercise helps release the punch. Music lifts the spirits. Outside interests occupy time, consume energy, and refocus thoughts. Being involved with others keeps "normal" in mind. Becoming enthusiastic about work or a hobby gives you other outlets.

Following are a few suggestions that will help you bring chaotic emotions under control. Basically these suggestions can be boiled down to a slogan: "Get a life." Tensions inside become less focused on one individual when the world doesn't spin around that person.

Do a daily check-off in your notebook as you follow through on each suggestion.

1. *Volunteer.* Help someone. Focus on what you give, rather than on what you get. Each day determine to do something for someone. Ask yourself, "What did I do for someone today?"
2. *Do some little, special thing for yourself each day.* Put a candle on the table, set out a bowl of fruit, put a flower by your sink, look at the stars, take a walk, and so on.
3. *Keep busy but not overwhelmingly busy.* Fill your time with a hobby, research a new interest, learn a new skill. Plan for new ventures to bring enthusiasm into your daily schedule.
4. *Say thank you five times during the day*—when you get up, at each meal, and before bedtime.
5. *Be calm and unafraid to say what you feel.*
6. *Say something positive each day to the people with whom you live or work.*

7. *Keep a journal.* Write down the good things about the day—a special call, an unexpected surprise, the sun coming up, whatever made you smile.

8. *Find concrete ways to meet your own emotional needs*— through fellowship with others who build and fill you, letters, telephone calls, a lunch with a friend.

9. *Read a positive meditation, quote, or joke each day.*

10. *Hug yourself and someone else at least once a day.*

11. *Do something outside.* Look at the stars, pick a flower, sit in the park and read the paper.

12. *Tell someone how special they are or what a good job they are doing.* Reflect on something good you can say to them or about them. Whom were you able to encourage?

13. *Sit quietly for a minimum of five minutes.* Refuse to allow your negative thoughts to control your quiet time.

14. *Write a thank-you letter to someone each week.* Thank someone for thoughts, acts, kindness, being who he is, caring ways, and efforts on your behalf.

15. *Exercise.* It's the key to controlling the punch of emotions and flooding your mind with good hormones.

Know Your Limits

Quite often a screwed-up person makes a mess of not only the relationship between you and her, but between you and others, because she butts in where she has no business being involved. She justifies the intrusion by relationship, caring, authority, right, insight, wisdom, or age. You must stand up for

> It's not wrong to have negative emotions; it's wrong to wallow and stay stuck in them.

yourself. Difficult relationships are caused by two people: the person who does wrong or irresponsible things and the person who allows it.

A young mother shared her conflict with her father—and the spin-off chaos it caused in her marriage. "My father does things that put my children in jeopardy, like driving his motorcycle with my three-year-old holding on to his back, or falling asleep at the lake while my little boy runs around on his houseboat. So unsafe. But when my husband told my father, 'No more!' I stood up for my father."

Confusion and conflicting emotions are enmeshed in difficult relationships. The father was irresponsible; the daughter was, likewise, irresponsible. She acted as a child, not an adult. *Gratitude should not be confused with turning your adult decisions over to someone else to make.* Knowing your boundaries and setting your limits will keep your emotions from taking over. There is no best way to handle the emotions that spin off difficult people, but there is one wrong way—stuffing your feelings. Having limits helps you know when to express what you feel.

Several people in the group with the young woman spoke up about their more positive interplay within their difficult relationships when they finally learned to handle the situations with maturity, rather than being childlike. Limits allow you to be an integral part of a relationship but not be emotionally consumed or controlled by its dysfunction: "I learned a long time ago to expect the bomb to drop at Thanksgiving time when our family gets together, so when my sister-in-law starts spinning off her criticism and attacks, I just get busy somewhere else. She's an unhappy person, and I am not going to play her game." "My wife nags me from the minute I get home until I leave. I used to stay at work as much as possible, but now I stop her harangues and,

Know your boundaries and set your limits.

though she acts as if she can't understand why I don't want her input, she shuts up." "I used to never open my mouth at work. I just did what I was told. But I stand up now if the issue is in my area of knowledge. I'm not pushy, but I don't get pushed around either."

Self-Control Wins

One of the great moments of your life will be the first time you are able to maintain control of your own actions and responses when a difficult person is on the rampage. You can do it if you back off! Refuse to argue. Set your limits. Stand as an equal who has the upper hand. You can care about and feel pity for this person whose ugly behaviors cause such chaos, but you don't have to let her control you.

Bo Jackson is one of America's great athletes. After winning the Heisman Trophy for his superior leadership as running back for Auburn University football, he went on to play both professional football for the Oakland Raiders and professional baseball for the Kansas City Royals. In his pep talks to youth, he tells of a defining moment in his life in seventh grade when, in a fight with a high school bully, he was knocked to unconsciousness. Bo said that when he came to, he was in such a rage he ran home, found his mother's handgun, and came back to find the kid who had humiliated him in front of his friends. He found him and raised the gun with every intention of killing the boy. As he was pulling the trigger, he heard Reason's whisper, "Bo, kill him and you'll spend your life in jail being beaten up by other bullies just like him. That's not the way to win." He turned the gun, and the bullet went into a tree.

Don't let your emotions put you in a prison. That's not winning.

Lifelines

- Progress flows from working with your emotions, as opposed to for your emotions.
- It's not wrong to have negative emotions; it's wrong to wallow and stay stuck in them.
- Know your boundaries and set your limits.

9

Let the Past Go

*When you can't change the direction of the wind,
adjust your sails.*

"I've had it," Frank announced. "Twenty years is enough time wondering if it is going to be hell when I get home. All I've been for a long time is a paycheck on legs. I can send money from anywhere and maybe have a shot at a new life."

Having proclaimed his intentions aloud, he stomped out of the barren desert in which he had survived two decades of longing for what wasn't, of wrestling with frustration, of grappling with anger. Frank joined the world of the divorced where half of all Americans have lived. His children became part of the three-fifths of all our children who live in homes with a single parent, a stepparent, or a "significant other."

Frank thought his leaving was a new beginning; instead, he found himself locked into the past on a continuing battleground in the present where the wounds include hurt feelings, resentments, and embittered relationships. As we talked, he expressed surprise that ten years after the parting of their ways, his experience confirmed research data that marital conflict is not terminated by divorce—changed, yes; ended, no.

I assured Frank that he was not unusual; the breakup of any significant relationship is rarely a ticket to freedom because, though most people leave difficult relationships, shouting, "I can't stand this anymore; let me out where I can breathe," they carry the hurt, injustice, wickedness, inequity, disrespect, and abuse along as part of their paraphernalia. They clutch them tightly, as if the very garbage they wanted to escape must be nurtured to justify their leaving the relationship.

Authors Wallerstein and Blakeslee share the discouraging data that flow from the breakdown of significant relationships. Their compilation of research shows clearly that the breakup of significant relationships puts people at much higher risk for both psychiatric and physical diseases, including every type of cancer.[1] Only 10 percent of people from broken marriage relationships responded that both people were living happier, fuller lives within a decade of the divorce. It was normal to find only one of the former partners in a stable second marriage, while the other tried and failed or never remarried. Nearly one-third of the children witnessed the intense bitterness of the parents toward each other. This had a negative effect on their feelings of security in all other relationships.

I shared with Frank that part of his problem was that, though he had reasoned through all the what ifs and tried to end his relationship as amicably as possible, he did what nine-tenths of all divorced people do—*he failed to let go*. He brought the baggage from his past, which he allowed inadvertently to distort his life in the present. His past bludgeoned his happiness by keeping him centered squarely on what had been lost, what should have been done, the dreams and hopes that were dashed, and the people who failed him. He knew that he needed to move on, but he was stalled, asking, "How can I move on when what has happened is so unfair?"

That is where most of us stall. We want to leave the hurts and wrongs behind. Our plan is to move on, or love "in spite of," or help without enabling, but the past keeps begging for our attention. Frank had spilled the milk, but instead of cleaning it up, for all these years he wallowed in it. Ten years after his divorce, he was tired. He no longer cared who was right and who was wrong. He just wanted to be happy.

The Root of Unhappiness

Longing is at the root of relationship problems. It spins off from four different mind-sets:

1. Reality is not the way we want it.
2. We want somebody or something to change.
3. We believe we are responsible to bring about change in someone or something.
4. We want to protect or rescue someone.

Longing is an obsession. You can't get your mind off a person or problem. You don't know what you can do, if anything, to make any difference, but you desperately want to help somebody or something change. You fantasize the possibilities, worry, and fret. Perhaps you love someone who is in trouble, someone who is out of control. His or her problem may be emotional, an eating disorder, gambling, alcoholism, or a lot of "isms" put together.

Or perhaps you are dealing with someone who is simply a jerk. His unreasonableness drives everyone else crazy. He may be self-centered or unable to keep commitments. He may have a negative attitude or show a constant lack of consideration or respect. If you don't adopt his opinion or give in, regardless of how it affects you, suddenly you are the bad guy. You are embarrassed or humiliated by the unreasonable, demanding, demeaning, or irresponsible attitude.

You may plaster excuses around the irregular behavior, wanting to protect someone from being hurt or not wanting to believe the truth because it hurts or is partially true. So you hide—and are inundated with longing. You say things like, "Daddy wanted to be here for your game but he had a problem at the office." "Mother isn't feeling well so she didn't want to come with us tonight." "Honey, your husband really loves you. He just doesn't understand how to treat a woman." "Son, your friend will invite you next time."

Longing is often grounded in incontestable needs, such as when parents long for their child to be drug-free. Often if our "ifs" were resolved, our life would be better:

- If Daddy would just come home, everything would be all right.
- If Mom would just get out and get involved, she would be happy.
- If my parents didn't have to work so hard, we would be able to do more things together.
- If my son studied, he could make As instead of Cs.
- If my brother would just help out with our parents, they wouldn't have to go to a nursing home.

- If my wife would just lose weight, our sex life could be great.

Unhealthy codependency that breeds longing is evident in relationships where rejection, rebellion, or clinging are found. Longing isn't productive. It hangs you up in "ifs." "If you believe that feeling bad or worrying long enough will change a fact or someone else's actions, then you are residing on another planet with a different reality system," wrote Dr. Wayne W. Dyer.[2]

What Can You Do?

Many family, office, organizational, or friend groups spin their lives around the actions of one of the members. Dealing with a difficult person can dominate the conversations and thoughts of the group. The family or group *does* need to talk about the difficult person, but it must be productive talk. Too often no positive action is taken because no one can see past the problem to figure out what to do. Healthy interconnectedness is the product of dealing with the problem, rather than ignoring it. Healthy families and groups learn how to be safety valves for each other, venting the pressure of dealing with the challenging member.

To stop the longing for what does not exist in screwed-up relationships, or to heal relationships that are beginning to skew, one must untangle from the emotions that swirl around or off a particular relationship. That process is called *detachment*. It basically means that you separate emotionally from the person around which your emotions swirl, in order to work on yourself, live your own life, feel your own feelings, and solve your own problems. Detachment is the goal of most recovery programs. Screwed-up relationships, like the screws in construction, are sometimes hopelessly entangled. Detachment separates you from the board into which you are screwed.

Frequently when I suggest to people that they detach from a person or problem, they recoil in horror, "Oh, no! I could never do that! I love him too much." Or they express their fears, "If I back off, he will not make it. He needs me. I must stay involved."

My response is, "But if detachment is the only way to bring stability and health to your relationship, do you still have to keep on the same course?"

Maybe understanding what detachment is not will take away some of your anxiety. Detachment is not:

- a cold, heartless, and hostile withdrawal
- a resignation, a despairing acceptance of anything life and people throw our way
- being blasé, naive, or blind to the problems
- being Pollyannaish, ignorantly blissful
- shirking true responsibilities
- necessarily a severing of the relationship

Detachment *is* releasing someone to be responsible for himself and to bear the responsibility of his own actions. Detachment gives us the objectivity necessary to look at our situation and glean from it the possible good, the lesson that can make the next steps in our walk more steady and focused, and can move us toward our goal. Detachment is ceasing to worry and changing our focus, perhaps heroically, from the other person to what is good for us in our life.

> Detachment is allowing others to be who they are, rather than who I believe they should be.

That's what Max had to do, even though when we first talked he didn't believe he could. "I just can't do it. My son won't make it. He's just not motivated to make the grades and keep up with his work unless I push. His whole life—and future of his family—may depend on our prodding and pushing. One of these days he will thank me, even if it's rough now."

Janice echoed the same, "My husband would be fat as a pig if I didn't stay on him about his eating. He needs my monitoring to keep his health."

I wondered if Max would not be better as his son's supporter than his antagonist. I wondered the same about Janice. Was she not married to an adult? Did he need a mother? It seemed so evident that Max's son and Janice's husband would be far more motivated if they felt it was their choice, rather than someone else's pushing, that got them to the goal. *Encouragement is important; support is crucial; pushing is dangerous.*

Help must keep a critical balance. Too little help and he may not make it. Too much help, and he may never grow up or may rebel against what feels more like control than help. Regardless of the composition of the other person's problems, if you gloss over them, the person will probably never change. But if you seek change actively, you may kill the relationship or become bitter if change doesn't occur. When someone is being pushed, it can be perceived as a put-down or a threat and can lead to clinging weakness, anger, rebellion, depression, or closed ears.

When we detach enough to stop pushing, we allow the person to decide what he wants to do. Melody Beattie, in *Codependent No More*, wrote, "sometimes detachment even motivates and frees people around us to begin to solve their problems. We stop worrying about them, and they pick up the slack and finally start worrying about themselves. What a grand plan! We each mind our own business."[3]

Consider the Lessons Life Teaches

When we begin to detach from the difficult person in our life, the longing often diminishes. As we begin to look at our situations objectively, we recognize that time does not stop longing; choice does, a choice that appreciates the lessons. It is choice that centers you on what you do have so you can stop longing for what you do not have. The past, good or bad, can be a primer for the present and future.

Frank learned: Life is full of growth lessons. We can't change some things, but we can learn from those and make the best of our situation. We can quit longing for *what is impossible* and choose the best from *what is possible*.

"My divorce didn't end my imprisonment. It ended when I said, 'No more. I've had enough regrets and sadness.' I determined to learn lessons from what had happened in my life. I was blessed to have a screwed-up relationship. Look at all I learned!"

The worst problem is always the one that belongs to "me." And if that problem hangs you up, regardless of its seriousness, you can be caught in a longing spiral that wants to suck the zest out of your life. I remember a vibrant, outgoing young woman, who was the seminar director in California, telling the group about a job-related move away from her parents and the community in which she had grown up. Even though the new community was safer, her home nicer, and the schools far better, she became so depressed, she attempted suicide. Many people related to her crisis. Through similar experiences that popcorned throughout the group,

> Centered on what you do not have, you will never see what you do have.

it was evident that staying stuck on what you do not have will prevent your seeing what you do have.

Like Frank we must stop and have a good self-talk, then restructure our course. Perhaps you need to sit down with yourself and ask several pertinent questions:

1. Is what I am doing in the relationship working?
2. Is the relationship important to me?
3. From observation of the past, what do I perceive is probable in the future?
4. How can I structure what I do to make the best of my situation?

Accept Your Reality

Accepting your reality is only possible when you see the possibilities and options that exist in the relationships that surround you. You may have tried to befriend an in-law, nurse a mother, support a child, shelter a friend, aid a father, back up an employee, or cry with a neighbor but found your advances either ignored or unwanted. Part of life is learning that not everyone wants the relationship you desire. You may long for your mother to mother you, your brother to be a pal, your child to express his caring, your children to make you grandparents. It may never happen, so accept the reality, even as you continue to be open to the possibility. To let go and move on, you must stop expecting something that is not going to happen.

This is where detachment comes in. Move on to fulfill your life with friends and family who do want to be part of your life. Sometimes unfulfilling relationships are just a matter of timing and heavy responsibilities. Sometimes the past obscures the possibilities for the present. Sometimes the person is unable to see you for the valuable individual you are. Sometimes you are wanting to help someone change who is quite content with who he is. Move on. Don't harden your heart if feelings are not mutual, but do free yourself from trying to earn the caring that should be a gift.

Detachment is both an action and an art. You are fortunate if you had people in your life who helped you learn the art of detachment. You are ahead in life's game if special people showed you how to care in healthy ways and to let go rather than hang on. But even if you had no mentor, you *can* extricate your mind, body, emotions, and spirit from the agony and longing that come with twisted relationships if you hold tightly to the lifeline that helps you accept your reality. As you gain strength, you may be a mentor to someone else who is trying to make it through her personal minefields.

The process of letting go is a bit clumsy at first, and you will experience much questioning and doubt. It's tough to let go when your fears are legitimate that someone will fall. It's agonizing if the choice to let go may mean the end of your relationship. It's hard to move on when the other person tries to keep you attached through guilt and manipulation. To extricate yourself from the pressure and control is an art when love stays at the helm.

> Real relationships are far more interesting than dreams.

Sometimes detaching in love is not possible. I believe it is better to detach in anger than to stay and exude poison toxins that destroy your emotional stability, peace, or other relationships. Mental distancing is crucial if you are to objectively discern ways to live in a less-than-perfect relationship that is important to you.

I know that many of you are suffering from years of physical or emotional abuse from people who did not consider your feelings. It is important that you detach immediately from an abusive relationship. Some of you have tried to hold too tightly or have nagged too much. Now is the time to change. This is your new beginning. You can break free of the cocoon that has trapped you in unhealthy behaviors or reactions. Perhaps through your freedom, others will be freed.

The butterfly doesn't spend its life regretting the time it spent eating the trees. It stops its old pattern, gets quiet within its cocoon, and then breaks free to spend the next part of its life bringing joy and beauty to its world as it spreads its wings. The experiences of your past, like those of the butterfly, can be used for good. Out of them you may develop empathy and understanding that will help you, like the butterfly, spread joy and beauty.

Perhaps the problem that is most likely to lock us into the past is our difficulty discerning if we are responsible for the breakdown in the relationship or if the other person is truly screwed up. We find ourselves courting guilt one minute and blame the next. It is frustrating because most damaged relationships are so entangled that "who-and-what" searches are nonproductive. Get on with the task. Twisted relationships are explosive. Failure to defuse the dynamite caps can cause your world to blow apart.

Lifelines

- Making the most of what we have turns it into more.
- Real relationships are far more interesting than dreams.

- Detachment is allowing others to be who they are rather than who I believe they should be.
- Centered on what you do not have, you will never see what you do have.

10

Buttons and Triggers

If you are exploding, it isn't because someone pushed your buttons, it's because you pulled your trigger.

Author Joyce Landorf's book *Irregular People* tells of her erratic relationship with her father. In her forties she was still being emotionally demolished by this man who was blind to his daughter's strengths, talents, skills, and successes. He was perfectly capable of seeing other people, himself, and his own needs with flawless 20/20 vision, and so his failure to affirm Joyce poured salt into her hidden wounds. She describes the experiences of being overlooked by him as akin to being shot down over a war zone, bailing out and landing in a minefield, having both legs blown off, and then not dying. She describes repetitive explosions at her father—during a phone call or visits, at lunch—and her genuine shock at her own behavior.

How could she be so out of control, feeling so furious, the adrenaline pumping through her veins, shaking with rage, hotly defending her position, and saying things she would deeply regret later on to a man she loved and admired? Why did every encounter turn into an insane rush down a dead-end alley? She remembers yelling as if the loudness would awaken her father's sensitivity, "Don't you realize that my books are far more famous than someone who just pays to have his own books published?" when her father raved on about a parishioner's self-published minibook. She asked herself, *"Why can't I have a loving conversation with this man?"*[1]

I read her book with great interest. The way she lays out the definition of an irregular person and describes the turmoil rings a bell with those who have experienced a turbulent relationship with someone they love. She described the feelings to a tee—the chaos, hurt feelings, and sense of failure. It was clear that she thought her father needed to change.

I wondered if Joyce was aware that if she chose wisely, her life would be better, whether her father changed or not. The person hanging on by the thread was not the irregular, off-the-wall father, but Joyce in whose weary hands lay the possibility of positive change. She needed real solutions, not the fairy-tale stuff where the frog turns into a prince after the princess kisses him.

Linda was in a similar situation. "I yelled at my father, 'Your priorities are screwed up. You never have time for anyone but yourself. You are a lousy father just like you've always been.' Then I packed up and went home. It was the same-old same-old. . . . It was just like I was a kid. We made a long trip home to be with my folks, but my father was busy. He had time for family meals but other than that was happy to scurry us off with Mom so he could do his thing alone. The more he said, 'Sorry, you go on. I have to finish this . . . ,' the more I felt the rage build. Retirement was no different than when he worked. He was busy with everybody and everything—but me."

Linda knew her behavior was childish. Being thirty-plus didn't stop her being hurt and angry at her father's lack of attention. "I've tried everything I can. What's wrong with me?" Linda's problem was simple for an outsider to discern: She was being controlled by buttons.

Buttons

Buttons are the danger signals that warn us of unresolved problems. They are part of our normal alarm system, like anger or adrenaline. They are the signals that say, "You have a problem." They are the guys out front who are shouting, "Don't stuff it! Deal with it now." They don't destroy your relationships; they point you in the direction of need so you can resolve the problems. Buttons aren't the bad guys; triggers are the killers. Your buttons are pushed and your reactive behavior pulls the trigger. *Whooammmm!* Your world blows apart.

> Buttons are the danger signals that warn us of unresolved problems.

Controlling triggers is possible if you respond to your buttons as opposed to reacting to them. How? Program your mind to act rather than react.

Prior to a full-blown earthquake, there are geological symptoms that act like buttons to warn that tension is escalating between the earth's massive plates of rock that float over a fluid core. Something eventually has to give to ease the tensions, or the ground shakes uncontrollably, splits occur, and anything in the way is splintered by the titanic power that explodes and implodes with incredible magnitude. The same is true of us as persons. We are conscious of only our surface lives, unable to see the powerful movements deep below our surface experiences. Tensions and pressures can develop that must

Act; don't react.

find release. They release in healthy ways or they implode and explode uncontrollably.

Buttons are the pressure valves that release built-up tension. These pressure valves are warning signals that major problems are buried that are struggling to get to the surface. Failure to respond to buttons by releasing the tensions causes the pressure to build, eventually triggering internal earthquakes. These internal shake-ups and meltdowns make it obvious that nursing resentment is as dangerous to love and relationships as is carrying a lighted match around dynamite caps. It's just a matter of time before everything blows up.

The surprise is that even with many symptoms clearly indicating unresolved problems, we are flabbergasted when the safety valves release a spurt of steam. Like Joyce Landorf or Linda, we feel dazed: Why did we respond to our screwed-up person the way we did? We are genuinely confused by our own repetitive reaction to the same old repetitive behavior. Someone needs to make a warning label: *If you notice warning buttons in your relationships, get help fast. The explosives you carry are highly inflammatory. If not defused, they will kill.*

Signs of Reactive Behavior

Do you remember the cartoon *The Road Runner*? It was a series of fight and flight incidents between a roadrunner and a coyote. Wile E. Coyote was ever hopeful of catching Road Runner, but his strategies always backfired, leaving him stunned, befuddled, or totally blown away.

In a difficult relationship, you don't want to be like Coyote, repeating the same reactive patterns. After Coyote was smashed or stepped on, Road Runner, like most difficult people, looked back only to assess the chaos, singing out, "Beep, beep," as he ran on. The point: Coyote never learned from his experiences.

It's important to recognize signs of reactive behavior so you can learn from your experiences. You can learn to identify symptoms and find healthy ways to resolve the tensions. Defusing the underlying problem before there is a major explosion is possible. Failure to address the buttons that try to point you to the problem areas builds the tension causing you to become bound and overreactive. Here are some indicators that your behavior has become button-bound:

> You overreact to any provocation, even to the point of rage.
>
> You feel manipulated, threatened, or controlled.
>
> You long for what you are not getting.
>
> Anger bursts forth, explosive and implosive.
>
> Emotions tailspin after confrontation—or even merely after being together.
>
> Issues from the past keep poking into the present.
>
> Immaturity abounds—stomping, pouting, tantrums, withdrawal.
>
> Chaos dominates the interactions.
>
> Your emotions seem out of control.

Reactive behavior is rooted in unrealistic or thwarted expectations. If after repeated difficult behaviors you say things like, "I'm sure this will never happen again," or "If I just work a little more (give more, do more, be more), I am sure things will change," you may be Coyotelike.

Mature adults find ways to free themselves from exploding off irregular behavior. I try to change from being critical of the difficult person to feeling sorry for him. Isn't it sad that someone you care about is limiting, possibly destroying, relationships by behavior that causes chaos? How awful to be so insecure, so cocksure, so caught in compulsive behaviors, so unwilling to change destructive patterns that a person stands as alone as an island, rather than joining hands in an alliance. Pity the person who drives others away by feigned illness, clinging dependency, fears, or efforts to control. Feeling sorrow instead of hurt turns angry fists into compassionate hands.

Relationships are not cartoons. Coyote couldn't choose to act. He was set on react. Fortunately, you can determine to make the best of what you have rather than spend another moment of your precious time wishing for what you don't have. Ask yourself if, in your efforts to obtain love, respect, or affirmation, you have become locked into responding to someone in patterns that are unhealthy. Think about whether you are repeating (Coyotelike) any of these behaviors that kill healthy interactions:

- saying *yes* when you want to say *no*.
- doing what you do out of fear
- fixing people's feelings
- fixating on someone else's life, as opposed to valuing your own
- assuming responsibilities because of obligation, rather than a caring or a desire to help
- obsessing about your weakness, inability, failure, or imperfection

> Feeling sorrow instead of hurt turns angry fists into compassionate hands.

- managing other people without their asking for your help
- longing for what is not
- dwelling in pity parties

Joyce Landorf deserved better treatment from her father. But her longing didn't change anything. Her Road Runner simply did his own thing and didn't intend to change his course. He probably looked back at his daughter, just as Road Runner looked at Coyote, wondering: *What is the problem?*

Stop Responding to Buttons

If you are twisted and tangled in a relationship mess, you can find ways to unscrew and untangle if you study your buttons and refuse to pull the trigger that pushes you into reactive behavior. Free yourself from the controls your SUP exerts. Stop the tug-of-war games and the dysfunction by understanding what can be understood, changing what can be changed, compromising when that is possible, negotiating the best within the circumstances, finding lessons in the difficult, and focusing on hope in the midst of the impossible.

Study your relationship. Evaluate the past lessons, determine a new course for the present, and move toward goals for the future. See the pluses and minuses. These are tools and lessons to be used for changing from negative directions to proactive behaviors. Think through these five questions and write your thoughts in your notebook so that you can refer back to your answers.

1. Why does your SUP irritate, hurt, or anger you?
2. Why do you think he acts this way?

3. What qualities do you appreciate in yourself—or in others—as the result of the irregular behavior of your SUP?
4. Do you grieve over the behavior or over what is lost in your life as a result of it?
5. What have you learned to do, or not do, as the result of the SUP's behavior?
6. Are there "gifts" in your life as the result of the behavior (your friends, more time with your children, time for your own priorities, and so on)?

A screwed-up person doesn't merely bug us—he wounds us, pulling out chunks of our heart. His poison darts dig deeper as the relationship skews. He does not hear or see our needs and rarely changes to meet them. But, just perhaps, he wonders about you and feels stung by your behavior: What's wrong? Why is she always so unappreciative? Can't she get her own life? Why is she always like a tiger in a cage?

Set your goal to control you, regardless of whether the SUP in your life changes or not. Five years from now you will be five years older, whether you attempt to change or not. Wouldn't it be great to be able to say, "I've changed. I'm free from the buttons that controlled so much of my life. I am no longer ready to explode at any moment"?

Lifelines

- Buttons are the danger signals that warn us of unresolved problems.
- Act; don't react.
- Feeling sorrow instead of hurt turns angry fists into compassionate hands.

11

Make Anger Your Ally

*In the confrontation between the stream and the rock,
the stream always wins—not through strength but
through perseverance.*

Anger is pervasive in screwed-up relationships. It is present
day after day, time and again. The wrong is so piled up or
horrendous, the control is so manipulative, or the hurt is so
devastating that it eats you alive until you are barely able to
speak the anger that fills your insides. It can stream forth in
cursing or attack through stony silence. Anger may drive
you to the point of wanting to kill. Some do. How do you
manage the feelings of anger that swell from living with a
screwed-up person?

"I couldn't stand it any longer. The only way out was to
kill them all—my wife and the kids. Divorce would not free

me. I'd never be free of the noose around my neck. It was like suffocating every day."

That's desperate. But anyone who has lived with a difficult person knows the feeling of hopelessness, of permeating anger, and of depressing inaction. What can be done? It's like being a rodeo rider. When you live with a bucking horse, you know you are going to be thrown. You hold on, make it through most of the rides, but inevitably you find yourself on the ground. Each time the horse bucks, the emotions pound, the adrenaline rushes. The more you tumble to the ground, the less aggressive the horse must be for your emotions to surge. And the older you get, the less willing you are to ride.

It's hard to want to continue a relationship with someone who bucks your every effort. It's tiring to hear the same old problems rehashed and rehashed. Discouragement rides alongside every encounter. The hope for keeping the fragile relationship together requires a twofold effort: managing your anger and taking control so that your hot wires aren't detonated.

Well-Managed Anger

Several years ago when Lee Iacocca was chairman of Chrysler, he addressed the graduating class at the University of Michigan. He lauded the virtues of well-managed anger.

> "Back in 1979," he said, "*The Wall Street Journal* advised me to let the Chrysler Corporation 'die with dignity.' I got mad. My colleagues in Highland Park got mad. Tens of thousands of Chrysler people all across America got mad. We got so mad that we banded together, we talked things over, and working together, we fixed what was wrong at Chrysler. We doubled

our productivity. We rejuvenated our factories. We cut our costs. We started building the highest quality cars and trucks made in America. In short, we turned things around."[1]

All of us get angry. Anger is part of us, like breathing—completely natural and perfectly legitimate. Anger is a physical state of readiness. Physiologically, when we get angry, adrenaline is released, our heart beats faster, our blood pressure rises, and we become more alert to threatening, frustrating, and fearful situations. Anger equips us to act decisively, which can bring about resolution and healing.

> To turn anger into an ally, partner with it.

Use your anger if you are in a crisis relationship as Lee Iacocca and the employees of Chrysler did. Get mad but harness your anger. *You* are at stake. *Your relationship* is at stake. Let your anger work for you by pushing you into action. Focus on managing the anger, rather than letting it manage you.

Although there are many ways to manage anger, in my experience over the past thirty years, I've noticed that most people tend to use one of the following five styles: exploder, victim, manipulator, rager, releaser. It is important to analyze your style. Recognizing how you manage your anger will encourage you to continue healthy patterns or change destructive ones. Appreciating the management style of others helps you team with them rather than being controlled or threatened by their anger. As you think about the five anger-management styles, consider whether your method of handling anger impedes or strengthens healthy problem solving.

Exploder

Everyone knows when exploders are angry. They blow up and blow out. They yell, break things, stomp, curse, and demand. Their mouth becomes a machine gun, shooting loud and deadly bullets. Exploders mull over their problem, determine a resolution, drop cloaked hints to clue you to their need; then when you don't pick up on what they want, they lose it.

To handle the spurts of steam or the uncontrollable rages of the exploder, allow the pressure to blow. Visualize the exploder as a pressure cooker, releasing the steam. Get involved when the explosion is going off and you will definitely be burned, so don't be defensive or try to correct misstatements during an explosion. But when it's over and before the pressure has built for the next explosion, sit down and talk. Find ways to get to the root of the anger.

Listen to what the exploder says: You never do what I need you to do . . . Why are you so hardheaded? . . . You made me lose my cool . . . You are eating me alive. Tell her you care. Ask her to talk to you as if you were a child who cannot understand the needs unless they are spelled out. The exploder learned early on her method for handling anger, but it can be unlearned if someone takes the time to help the exploder learn a new anger-management style.

Whether the exploder changes or not, you can stop being reactive. Get out of the way, let it blow, and go on. Caution: If the verbal explosion becomes physical abuse, protect yourself and those in your care. Leave if possible until the explosion is over.

Victim

Victims are the usually low-key people who never get visibly angry but are often chronically depressed. They suffocate their spirit by self-belittlement and blame. They layer themselves in guilt and turn their anger at their failures into self-flagellation. They have not learned to express their emotions, so their anger remains bottled up and unresolved. It spurts forth in psychosomatic problems such as hypertension, headaches, and colitis and in suffocating, clinging behaviors that cause others to want to flee.

Exploders and victims come from the same mold. They both learned in childhood that anger was bad. They were taught that good children are self-controlled, forgiving, and obedient, not angry. But this left them confused about how to express their frustrations. Their anger becomes like a Coke bottle that has been shaken and is ready to explode when the cap is opened. Exploders explode outwardly, hitting whatever is in the way; victims implode inwardly, taking the abuse personally. Neither expression is healthy. Both cause people around them to avoid the relationship.

Victims' spurts of anger can be seen in sad days, down periods, and self-directed abuse sessions when you hear self-incriminatory statements such as, I never do it right . . . I'm so sorry . . . I apologize. Their implosion, like the exploders' explosion, controls their mind and will, leaving them limp, useless, and devastated, but still cooking with pressure building toward another crisis.

Victims are draining because one tends to try to bolster them up, help them see the sunshine, give them positive one-liners. But you can't get through to them until the pity party is over. Then you might say, "I'm sorry this is a bad day for you." Stay objective. Don't allow a victim to cling or control. Don't correct. Do state the truth: You are a great person. I care about you very much. Later, when she can hear, is the appropriate time to talk about the problem that set off the implosion and about anger management, not while she is imploding. Statements such as, "You are not managing your anger well; you are turning it on yourself," will do no good. It's all right to feel sorrow for victims, but don't be dragged down. They choose the way they manage their anger.

Manipulator

Manipulators are "I never get angry" people. They exhibit superior self-control—never rage, raise their voice, or use curse words. Yet as anger begins to seethe, they target their victim with guilt, sarcasm, and innuendos. Manipulators are unable to recognize their own anger. They don't see that their snide remarks, put-downs, sneaky tricks, or "jokes" are really expressions of their anger. They say, "Just kidding," or "I didn't mean anything by it," and think they are speaking the truth.

As children, manipulators may have been unable to get their needs met by simply asking, so they learned to maneuver on the sly to get what they wanted. Perhaps they could get attention only by being sick, or get the toy they wanted only by striking a bargain.

And now in adulthood, rather than negotiating adult to adult, they use whatever device available—authority, money, power, dependency—to get what they want. Manipulators don't realize that as adults they are expected to talk to people as adults and interact with integrity.

Rager

Ragers nurse anger. They bite you with their words and eyes. They suspect the worst, see no good, and pound whatever is nearby. Their seething is evident in their critical remarks, body language, or vicious attacks. They rage at everyone or at specific targets, but never at themselves.

Ragers, like manipulators, learned their style for expressing anger at the knee of their parents. They grew up under the thumb of controlling parents, and their anger now burns at the world in general. They have become so negative about life that nothing pleases them; everything makes them angry, and they want everyone to know. "Do what I say or you will be smashed," is the threat that speaks loudly from their demeanor.

Releaser

Use and release is the way to manage anger successfully, especially in a relationship with a screwed-up person. *Feel it; use it; let it go.* The emotion is expressed and released. Any of the other methods of dealing with anger just make a toxic relationship more toxic.

Releasers use anger as their ally. They are not afraid of anger, nor do they try to deny it. They recognize anger for what it is—a signal. This encourages them to discern the source of the problem, energize, act on the need, and then let go of the anger. They see anger as a friend, a tool, and a necessary part of their healthy emotions.

Feel it; use it; let it go.

Take Control

Anger is a good emotion when it is under control; it is destructive when anger controls you. It's a lot like money in your hand. Hold the money and it's unusable. Throw it carelessly away and it is of no value. Its value is released as you spend it productively. Likewise, the goal of anger management is to stop fearing anger, use it productively, and release it. It must be acted on to be of value.

Anger as an ally will do the following:

- alert you to a problem
- energize you toward a goal
- bolster your determination and perseverance
- prod you to appreciate your own needs
- keep you from feeling overwhelmed
- let you know that the problem is yours to handle
- fortify your resolution
- act as a thermostat for other emotions

If you are angry because of an ongoing problem, stop dead in your tracks. This is your signal. If all your reasoning, tactics, maneuvering, begging, or yelling have not changed the difficult person's actions, quit fighting the wind. If that person hasn't responded, it's because she doesn't want to change—regardless of what is promised. No matter how unfair, you are forced to either live with it or leave. *Your* power is found in what *you* do. Exploding, being a victim, raging, or manipulating through anger is not a good choice.

It's often difficult to control your anger when you are dealing with your SUP. This is because she seems to know what will set you off and has no qualms about doing it. Your SUP also resists making changes that would make your relationship more compatible. The frustrations that you feel can easily escalate into anger. Here are some things that your difficult person may be doing that make it a challenge for you to control your anger.

- using unfair tactics
- trying to justify wrongs
- making choices that affect you or those you care about without any input from you
- twisting your words

- not trying to change problem behavior
- not listening
- avoiding compromise or negotiation
- feeling the end justifies the means

Recognize your hot wires, the things that set you off and then expect your SUP to play those wires like a violin. Expecting what will probably happen keeps you from being reactive. If you know the maneuvers and your reactions to them, you can distance yourself so that you are not controlled and frustrated by these tactics. This allows you to address the problem without complicating it with uncontrolled anger.

At a wedding I attended, the grandmother of the bride reminisced, "I hope these kids are smarter than I was. I've been a world-class crab for most of my marriage. It took almost crashing and burning before I saw the picture. I spent a lot of years trying to change everyone and everything. I was angry at the world. I was the one who needed to change! I needed to get a life!" she said.

Getting a life gives you handles to shift your attention away from your personal problems and focus on the options within your own grasp so that you do not stew in your own pressure cooker. The choice to get a life heightens your awareness that you are a unique, separate, and distinct individual, responsible for your own happiness. You can seethe in anger or do something productive with it, regardless of what others choose. Use the following techniques to take the oomph out of your anger and put the power back into being a productive person.

Techniques to Take the Oomph out of Anger

- Think through the "what ifs" so you will not be reactive.

- Take time for yourself so tension can be released in positive ways.
- Treat yourself by playing occasionally.
- Laugh.
- Take time to see and enjoy life's treasures—the baby's smile, the dew on leaves, stars, lightning bugs, croaking frogs.
- Explore new hobbies.
- Be a friend and find a friend.
- Find a support group or mentor.
- Stop waiting for someone outside yourself to fulfill you.
- Do a blessings diary, listing the good and special things that happen each day.
- Spend some moments each day in quiet—even if it's in a car.
- Listen to uplifting music.
- Read uplifting literature.
- Control your thoughts.

Lee Iacocca got mad. He found strength as he bonded together with those around him to keep Chrysler alive. Find a source of strength outside your relationship. Sure, your husband should make you happy. Your children owe you. Parents are supposed to be nice. Bosses should respect their employees. So? Screwed-up relationships stay screwed up because no one will budge. Use your anger to get off your duff and make a difference.

Lifelines

- To turn anger into an ally, partner with it.
- Feel anger; use it; let it go.

Fight Fair
with Unfair People

Love is what holds hearts together when minds disagree!

E. V. Hill, a prominent black minister in the Watts area of Los Angeles, was summoned by J. Edgar Hoover to Washington, D.C. The Black Panthers, a radical terrorist group, were holding New York City hostage, threatening to blow up all the bridges if any cars tried to cross. Police imposed curfews, roadblocks, and massive manhunts; yet scouring the city had not turned up the terrorists. Hoover pleaded with Reverend Hill to appeal to the black community to stop the Black Panthers' siege. E. V. Hill looked at Hoover in disbelief. "Mr.

Hoover, how many did you say were involved in the Black Panther movement—eighty-nine? Eighty-nine are holding two million people hostage? How is that possible?"

Experience with a screwed-up person might shed light on Reverend Hill's question. It wasn't the number of people; it was their tactics that held the city captive. Fear put New York City into captivity, not eighty-nine people. Difficult people play a psychological game that skirts the rules—*all is fair, anything goes, and nothing is off-limits*. This makes it difficult for those of us who were taught to play fair, be nice, don't bite, say you're sorry, and turn the other cheek. Early on, we learned that nice people abide by the rules and principles of good behavior. That leaves us ill-prepared to fight with screwed-up people.

Mind Games

Fighting with screwed-up people plays with your head. The New Yorkers were not captive physically; they were captive in their minds. They feared being on a bridge or subway that might blow up, being outside where a bullet might target them, and being in the center of the limitless possibilities of harm. They feared being hurt. Isn't that why it's so hard to deal with a difficult person? You don't want to be hurt. You don't want to lose something that is important to you—money, love, power, respect, security. Fear is holding you hostage and making the SUP seem bigger than life, more powerful than death, and more threatening than your ability to overcome. When winning becomes more important than playing by the rules, anything goes. Reasonableness, fairness, and accepted logic are left by the wayside. The difficult person's objective is to win, to be on top, not become your friend or appease your ego. Self-worth is driven by being the big dog, the one in charge. Can you imagine a conference call to the Black Panthers?

> The police: "Sirs, we want you to understand our viewpoint. There are a lot of innocent people who could get hurt. You are not being fair."
>
> The Black Panthers: "So?"

Emotionally healthy people find it very difficult to play games with people who refuse to abide by the rules. Knowing what to expect helps you deal with the irregular tactics of your SUP and plants you in the real world where screwed-up people rarely choose to play fair. The fantasy that you will be heard or that there will be compromise in areas that are driving you nuts gives way to the reality that regardless of your effort, there may be no change.

So how do you fight with unfair people? How do you resolve differences when unfairness makes you want to close down your bridges and huddle in a fortified bunker? How do you keep from responding in kind, relegating fairness to the trash heap?

The best advice for fighting with a screwed-up person is simple: DON'T. You cannot be logical with an illogical person. The only way to win is to never, under any circumstances, get pulled into an argument. If you fight, you lose! Questioning choices questions integrity. Suggesting different ideas implies lack of intelligence. Seeking negotiation disputes power. Wanting compromise conveys weakness.

Screwed-up people often win because:

> Their tactics don't follow the rules.
>
> Confrontation degenerates into dogfights.
>
> The real issues are avoided.

Something essential is withheld until the opponent gives in.

Tactics

Screwed-up people don't fight unless they have you over a barrel. They mean to show you who is in control and who is superior. They know they will win because you need what they have. They know others who need them will support their actions, even when their behavior is wrong. A difficult person reasons that no one would have problems if everyone did it *my* way.

"I couldn't believe my ears. I was pelted, beaten, cut up, and shredded—all in five minutes. My brother twisted what I said, put words in my mouth, discredited my work, belittled my efforts, and then started on me personally, accusing and blaming. He sliced me open and diced me to pieces. Then what I did was unbelievable. I kissed his ring. I need his help, so I crawled out like a whimpering, bloodied dog."

To compound the agony, often those around point their finger in derision at the victim. "You brought on the storm. You know he's not reasonable. Why did you stir the pot by talking to him like he was? He doesn't mean half of what he says. He would never do anything to hurt you."

The victim feels helpless. Those around compound the abuse because they too are needy. Hopelessness and resignation reign. "I'm going to forget it. What can I do? What choice do I have? I'm stuck."

Though difficult people come in every shape and size and in either gender, they all fight with similar tactics because, regardless of the maneuvers, the goal is the same: control that wins. Here are some of the tactics that screwed-up people use.

They fight to win, regardless of what it takes, using weapons of emotional destruction, such as guilt, anger, denial, withdrawal, pain, rejection, and criticism. They focus on what they know are your buttons and triggers and will harp on your inadequacies. Typically they refuse to hear what you have to say. If attacks on your character don't achieve the desired outcome, they will aim their attack at others for whom you care.

Arguments are not logical. SUPs change their argument in midstream, do a complete turnabout, if necessary, to keep the upper hand. They disregard and disparage. They deny they said or did what you know they said and did.

> Center on the goal of healthy resolution and don't give in to a dogfight.

Their comments make it clear that they believe you are not able to understand the issues as they can.

The tactics of screwed-up people are designed to put the onus of blame, guilt, and unreasonableness on you, the hostage. You are the culprit for forcing them to do whatever they did. They justify their behavior by their "concern" for you and their desire for you to benefit from their superiority, their religious insights, and their political understanding. They never apologize or acknowledge any wrong unless an apology will further their control. Actually, they may be unaware of their unfair maneuverings and shocked by what they consider your ingratitude and personal attack.

It is hard to stay focused on the point of the conflict when the other person changes his argument midstream, refuses to acknowledge what he just said, twists your words, debates the subject by debating your intelligence or worth, and brings up issues from the past. Yet to resolve the problems, you must not get sidetracked by the tactics. Center on the goal of healthy resolution and don't give in to a dogfight.

Jimmy Carter's wife, Rosalynn, was interviewed on the Phil Donahue show. Mr. Donahue was grilling her about a decision her husband had supported. He soliloquized for five minutes in a philosophical, erudite debate against President Carter's choice. He ended by asking, "Now what do you think?"

She looked at him and brightly said, "I don't have any idea what you are talking about. I just know Jimmy always tries to do the right thing." The audience broke into laughter, he was speechless, and she ended the debate then and there. She refused to get into a dogfight with Donahue.

Recognizing Our Own Power

The greatest hope for change in a difficult relationship begins when someone changes tact. Don't spend your life running on the same old track, bowing, scraping, begging, trying to earn, and eventually surrendering all you have to win something that should have been a gift—acceptance and appreciation. You may be doing the same thing. It may help you to know you lose less when you aren't afraid of losing. You lose who you are when you shy away from the issues, because what you avoid controls you. Power in mind games comes from facing the issues squarely, being straightforward, and not arguing.

> You lose less when you aren't afraid of losing.

It's important to recognize three relationship realities:

1. You lose less when you aren't afraid of losing.
2. You lose when you try to avoid issues.
3. What you avoid controls you.

Survival Tactics

The psychological war with a screwed-up person puts most of us at a disadvantage before we even start. We begin discouraged, for we know what it is to stick our foot in our mouth, allow our emotions to control our words, and get off on tangents instead of staying with the issues. We've been there and blown it. We get riled just thinking of the problems, because overcoming set patterns seems so hopeless.

Study, preparation, and careful execution of a plan are crucial if you are to keep from being sucked into the power of a difficult person who refuses to play by the rules. Preparation helps you distance yourself so that your emotions do not interfere with your rational choice of the best option for resolving conflict.

Talking through the Problem

To set the stage for talking through a problem with your screwed-up person, you should do the following:

- Arrange a quiet time to discuss a specific issue.
- Agree on the rules.
- Use the speaker-listener technique where each person takes turns talking and listening; the listener repeats back what he or she heard.
- Separate the problem discussion from the problem solution.
- Agree on a resolution and set a time to meet again to discuss progress in establishing the compromises.

You may not be able to get a screwed-up person to sit down in a quiet place, stay attentive, listen as well as speak, and work toward a healthy resolution. But you can try. Even if all the conditions are not perfect, you can control your own actions. Stop yourself, shut your mouth, and listen when the person interrupts or wants to speak. Even if you don't agree, listen without interruption. In a soft tone correct untruth. Say something similar to these noncombative and nonchallenging statements, as you clearly and quietly restate the truth:

- I'm sorry, but I do not feel like you think I do . . .
- What I really said was . . .
- I appreciate what you said, but I have not found that to be correct . . .
- Could we get back to the subject?

Talk in terms of "we" when you refer to your goals and partnership. Use "I" statements to show your commitment to the process. Your words should express goodwill, hope, and caring, even as they convey your concerns.

- We surely can find a way to be good friends . . .
- We have a lot in common . . .
- I want to . . .
- I hope we can . . .

Ask questions that encourage the other person to express his goals for the relationship. You need to understand what is possible between you. Avoid browbeating, illuminating all the wrongs.

- What do you think we might do to have less conflict?
- What are your goals for our relationship?
- What would make you feel better about what we do together?
- Do you really believe this would work?

Some therapists encourage those whose relationship seems stalemated in conflict to move on, not looking back. They argue that if you haven't been heard before, you won't be heard now. But if you are in the relationship for the long haul, what do you have to lose by trying to resolve problems, except an unhappy status quo? Limping along is not acceptable to someone who wants to live victoriously. You need to find a new way to bring resolution to differences.

> Preparation is the key to having a productive conversation.

Confrontation

Confrontation may be the new tactic you need to use. Confrontation isn't threatening if you follow simple ground rules. You lay out the problem; you state what you will no longer do or accept if you are to continue the relationship. It is not negotiable. Confrontation is not argumentative or reactive. It is proactive.

Using confrontation, you:

- face the problem
- consider the options
- recognize the pluses and minuses of each option
- choose a course of action
- don't argue the decision

Perhaps you are thinking: Won't work. I've tried that and it was a disaster. He won't hear me. The old behavior will just keep going on.

It is possible that the reason confrontation did not work previously is because you allowed the confrontation to evolve into an argument. You didn't lose because you confronted; you lost because you argued.

Remember, the purpose of confrontation is not to:

- retaliate
- punish
- put the other person down
- dump your anger

The purpose of confrontation is to:

- confront the problem
- try to resolve the internal chaos
- determine if you can continue the relationship
- overcome your fear of being yourself with your difficult person
- tell the truth

Enter any confrontation with an SUP knowing what you avoid controls you. Timing is critical

> **What you avoid controls you.**

to success. Choose a time when there will be no interruptions, no phone calls, no people, no kids. You need to be calm, not rushed, and so does the person with whom you are trying to resolve issues. Screwed-up people use business, limited time, rudeness, and interruptions to keep others off balance. Expect such behavior and don't allow it to bother you. Think about the timing so you know when to confront and when to quit.

STEP 1: FIGURE OUT THE CONTROL TECHNIQUES

Screwed-up people have identifiable techniques they use to get their way. These tactics are like their personalized hammer. Your SUP will control you through his words or actions unless you can stand back and determine not to be drawn into conflict by such tactics. If you see the tactic as a battle maneuver, you will be less likely to be knocked off your feet or pounded into the ground.

One of the most clever manipulative techniques I've seen was used by a person who moved around his hometown in a wheelchair to gain sympathy and attention. Out of town he walked, danced, and cavorted without the chair. When the truth was known, the chair no longer had the same power to arouse sympathy. Recognizing the "chair" that your difficult person uses with you will destroy its power to control you.

Recognize the control techniques your difficult person uses:

- It may sound like, "I'm too tired, too sick, too busy, not able, need you to do it; I don't have enough money, talent, or ability."
- It may be compulsive behaviors—drinking, sex, food addictions, illness.
- It may be irritating behaviors, such as your partner refusing to be on time until you are screaming, "I'm leaving!"
- The person may use withdrawal of whatever you hold dear or need.
- The behavior may include pouting, whimpering, pleading, stomping, demanding, rewards, withdrawal, avoidance, and silence.
- It often includes verbal assault and freely using negative comparisons and guilt. Some difficult people are brash and loud; others are subtle and quiet.
- It probably includes cutting jokes and put-downs.

- Interruptions that short-circuit the expression of opinions and ideas are to be expected.

STEP 2: PRACTICE BEING OBJECTIVE

The relationship will get worse on its own unless intentional efforts are made to make it better. Count on that. The secret to not being caught by dysfunctional behavior is to expect it. Looking objectively at past experiences can desensitize you to control maneuvers so that the problem can be discussed rationally. Logic requires a third-person, objective view of the situation. Don't let a tactic tie up your emotions so that you are unable to distance yourself from the fray.

Write down your observations about the relationship interactions in the past. Remember the bitter disappointment of an argument with your difficult person and how the intention to resolve a problem turned into a battleground. Use that knowledge to guide you to better approaches. Think about the methods that got nowhere, the words that were not heard. Think about words or behaviors that escalated the effort to resolve issues into a worse mess. Remember what made the difficult person feel cornered and become vicious in a counterattack or become so crushed that he wallowed in self-pity, threatened to jump off a bridge, or even became nearly catatonic.

Write down the key control phrases that your difficult person uses, such as:

I have tried to do so much for you.
I wouldn't tell you these things if I didn't care.
You can't understand.

To be objective, you must do four things: visualize, desensitize, detach, and practice.

1. *Visualize* the worst possible scenario and then decide how you will deal with it. Visualize faces—furious, disbelieving, belligerent, hurt. Visualize actions and responses.

2. *Desensitize* yourself by saying out loud what the other person may say. Decide how you will respond. Sometimes it helps to role-play with a friend who is familiar with your situation. Tell her to pull out all the stops and say the worst things imaginable. Answer back calmly and objectively. Stay focused on what you want to say. If you feel uncomfortable sharing with a friend, role-play with a chair. Talk to the chair as if you are the difficult person, then switch roles by sitting in the chair and talking back to your difficult person. You can use props—hats or scarves—to make the role-playing feel real. Think through what may happen so you can defuse the power and the fear of hurtful words or actions.

> Confrontation is not negotiation or argument.

3. *Detach* by keeping the goal in mind: your freedom to choose. Detachment is aerial view; it's how to be objective. It is the ability to be part of the dialogue without being emotionally captured. Success with an SUP depends on this ability to separate yourself from the SUP's tactics. As you participate in the dialogue, keep foremost in your mind that this person is not bigger or more powerful than life. And ultimately you choose what you will do.

4. *Practice* what you intend to say until you can say it succinctly and without rancor or anger. Remember, you are confronting. You aren't negotiating. You are stating your terms and determining your options. Prac-

tice being in control and not controlled by the other person's actions.

Put It to Work

To heal a damaged relationship—to partner—never make statements that leave out hope. Remind yourself—and your difficult person—that you are talking about this because you care. You aren't trying to change him; you are trying to find what will make your interactions feel good for both of you. Acknowledge that he may not feel the tension that you feel. Keep pointing out that you care, you are sorry, you intend to stay, but you want peace.

It is common for a difficult person to act as though he has no idea what your problem is. He may suggest any negative feelings are solely on your part. This is a tactic that keeps the person from addressing the issues. The suggestion that it is your problem implies that you should shape up, realign your focus, or get a better attitude. You may be unable to break through this facade, but you can try.

> Win war games by convincing the warrior it is in his best interest to stop playing.

Remember, in the long run you win war games by convincing the warrior it is in his best interest to stop playing. It's important to remember that though screwed-up people may not be concerned with what's best for you, they are concerned about what's best for their own good. If your goals are perceived to further their self-interest, they will be less combative. So *figure out how you can make what you need feel like what they want.* Self-interest can make a strange bedfellow.

The goal of sitting down to talk through problems with your difficult person is to find a way to get along, to be a team, to be supportive of each other, to partner. The change in you may seem like a challenge to him. He may attack verbally; withdraw; assail your competency, ability, and intelligence; and bemoan your ingratitude. The important thing at this point is your response.

Practice answering with such lines as these:

- Name calling won't get us anywhere.
- I'm sorry you do not understand my point. Let me state it again.
- You agreed to hear me out.
- There must be a problem, or I wouldn't be here and you wouldn't be so defensive.
- I care, or I wouldn't talk to you about this.
- I believe you want a good relationship too.
- I know you are a caring person, and I am sure your goal is the same as mine—to support each other.
- I won't accept your labeling.
- Please let's keep to the topic.
- This does not involve others; we are talking about you and me.
- It's not okay for you to talk to me that way.
- Let me state this again, because I do not believe you heard me.
- Why are you responding with such rage?

Letter Writing

Some counselors suggest writing a letter to the person with whom you struggle. Danielle wrote a letter. It was easier to write what she felt than face her estranged brother. She organized her thoughts and wrote graciously, tactfully, and succinctly her need. Unfortunately, she forgot that she was not dealing with someone who would recognize the effort, appreciate the concern, and want compromise. Her brother read between the lines, misinterpreted her comments, resented her suggestions, and felt threatened by her audacity. He ignored her, misquoted her, and used the letter as a missile to demoralize her.

I suggest you write letters to reasonable people. Even write letters to organize your own thoughts. But confronting issues with a screwed-up person demands a face-to-face encounter. It's more difficult to misconstrue words when you hear the inflections. Misstatements and misinterpretations can be corrected when you sit across a table from each other. But unfortunately, even face-to-face, many SUPs simply twist your words and use them against you.

Advice and Criticism

Advice and criticism are like two knives that can tear apart relationships. The first time Jane and I talked, she was ready to ask her mother to stop her visits. Her mother saw nothing but bad in the man she loved and the lifestyle she led. She vented to me, decrying the invasion of her privacy, yet she loved her mother. It took time for her to be ready to transition from reactive to proactive with the difficult person in her life.

"Mother puts me on the defensive from the moment she enters my door. 'Jane, these plants are dying from lack of attention . . . I'll do your dishes, since every dish you have must be in the sink . . . I don't know how you find anything in this refrigerator . . . If you cook like this every night, your husband is going to die early from a heart attack . . . How can Frank find his way to the bedroom without breaking his neck with so much clutter in the hall? . . . Do you always go out looking like this? . . . Your sister's husband is nice to me . . .'"

Mutual regard is impossible when one person mistreats another and that person allows it. Relationship tension will escalate unless some constructive action is taken. Be aware that countering a difficult person's behavior with anything but approval will be perceived as an affront. Three options exist to handle criticism and unwanted advice:

1. Continue the relationship but ask that advice be given only when requested.
2. Cease activities that tempt the person to criticize or give advice.
3. End the relationship.

Perhaps you can practice with a friend, sharing the concerns that spring from your difficult relationship. For instance, Jane might say: "Mother, I need you to treat me like an adult. Your help makes me feel criticized and angry. I want a close relationship, but I need to know that you respect my right to be who I want to be."

The next time Jane's mother visited, she arrived laden down with food. "I knew with all the running around you do that you wouldn't have time to fix something healthy for your husband to eat, so I cooked all day." Jane thanked her mother and then asked her to sit down and have a cup of coffee with her. As they chatted, Jane let her mother know that she wanted their relationship to grow. She said something like this: "Mother, I love you enough to want to share with you a problem that I feel is hurting our relationship. I want your support, but your constant advice makes me feel you don't trust my judgment. It is driving a wedge between us. These are the options I think we have if we are to grow to be friends, which is what I really want . . ."

Jane's mother reacted angrily. Jane was tempted to counterattack. It is very important to stick to your nondefensive stance, or you will hand over your newly won power. Instead, say things like the following:

- Would it be better for us to talk about this later when you are not crying?
- I hoped you could talk to me rather than clamming up. It will be hard for us to be close if you try to punish me with your silence.
- I am willing to talk about other options, but I won't allow you to insult me.

Jane's mother stormed out—hurt, angry, and saying she wouldn't be back. She shoveled guilt-laden phrases on to Jane. But Jane did not buckle. Reestablishing the relationship ground rules in difficult relationships is crucial for emotional health. The important statements she made expressed love, concern, and limits. "I love you. I'm sorry, but our interactions are not good for either of us."

> Saying *I care about you* and *I'm sorry* keep differences from becoming irreconcilable.

The good news is that over time tension eased and Jane's mother did resume her visits and she stopped her criticism. *I care about you* and *I'm sorry* are two statements that keep differences from becoming irreconcilable. A little love goes a long way to win over difficult people, especially when limits must be set.

Long-Term Control

Following a confrontation (remember, not an argument), you may feel that you finally have the upper hand. It feels good to have expressed yourself without anger. You are exhilarated that you gained the courage to set limits and boundaries. But you may also feel severely off balance and anxious about what is going to happen next. Do nothing. Wait it out. Ultimately both the high and low will dissipate, and you'll enjoy a steadily increasing sense of well-being and confidence with your newly gained freedom.

Give-and-take is a part of all healthy relationships, but there must be limits. It can't be all give on one side and all take on the other. In handling conflict, your job is to not get pushed back into your old reactive and defensive patterns, regardless of what your difficult person does. Love is what holds hearts together when minds disagree.

Lifelines

- Center on the goal of healthy resolution and don't give in to a dogfight.
- What you avoid controls you.
- You lose less when you aren't afraid of losing.
- Preparation is the key to having a productive conversation.
- Confrontation is not negotiation or argument.
- Win war games by convincing the warrior it is in his best interest to stop playing.
- Saying "I care about you" and "I'm sorry" keep differences from becoming irreconcilable.

13

How Can I Ever Forgive?

*Injuring your enemy puts you below your enemy;
revenging an injury makes you even; forgiving it sets
you above.*

The elderly, frail couple looked straight at the physician.
"How many times are we supposed to forgive?" This day
their two grandchildren had been adopted by strangers. Their
only child granted adoption rights of her two children to a
couple she did not even know. She didn't give the children
away because her parents had failed to help or because she
was physically unable to care for them. She gave away the
kids because she didn't want the responsibility. Their daughter's choice had stolen another part of their hearts. This was
another dumping time, another crisis, another loss. "How
many times," they wanted to know, "is enough?"

If their question is really, How many times do you get back into the game with help? there is no easy answer. Though help should have limits, it also has variables. If the question is, How many times should I forgive? there is an answer. Forgive as many times as you are hurt, wronged, stomped on, or crushed. Why? Because forgiveness may help the other guy, but its primary gift is to free you. Don't mix the question of helping with the question of forgiving. The formula for forgiveness is simple: *If you are hurt or angry, forgive.*

> The primary gift of forgiveness is to free the one who forgives.

It may be easy to brush off the crazy or mean behavior of someone who is not significant in your life. You may even be able to laugh at her. But negative, hurtful acts committed by a person about whom you care threaten your happiness. They are more than simple acts; they are dangers. Slowly, if hurts fester and stew, they act like a rising fog in front of your windows. The light is blocked, and soon it is difficult to see anything but the fog. It's a deadly process that creeps in through the nagging thoughts that cling to a wrong. *Ouch! I did not deserve such treatment. They are so unfair.* The twinkle fades, the laughter dwindles, and steps become heavy. Do whatever it takes to stop the process. Change what you can. Accept that which you cannot change. Forgive it all.

A Determination

Forgiveness is a determination to be free! I won't let what someone else does destroy me, regardless of how I am affected. Whether you forgive or not has nothing to do with the seriousness of the abuse or wrong; it has everything to do with whether you want to be free or prefer to carry the burden. Forgiveness is a choice that begins with a discovery—a discovery that the grudge you nurse in your mind, regardless of its size, is the heaviest weight you can carry in this world.

In the movie *The Mission* a slave trader in Brazil is converted to Christianity. He is convicted of his horrific atrocities committed against the local Indians—the murder, rape, and inhumanity of his trade. To do penance he drapes himself in chains and walks, burdened by the weight, to the church at the top of a mountain. In a poignant scene the ex-slave trader is struggling up the mountain. He is barely able to put one foot in front of the other. His life is in obvious peril as he falls near the rock ledges of the narrow trail. As he struggles to raise himself up, an Indian jumps out of the bushes with his machete raised high over his head. The observers gasp as the sharp knife comes down. It appears to be justice meted out by an Indian who had reason to want this man dead. The knife hits its mark—the chains. They snap, break free, and clang off the precipice into the canyon below. The slaver is free of his chains, his bondage. And the Indian is free too. His ability to forgive has freed him to act humanely and to live without the burden of vengeance.

Forgiveness happens when a mental lightbulb turns on. She may drive me crazy, but I am the one who carries the baggage everywhere I go. Forgiving is a choice that gets rid of the baggage. It turns mere survival into victorious living as it cuts you loose from the power of your abusers and your desire to do them wrong. Failure to forgive locks you into a self-focus that pleads for restitution and revenge. Negative thoughts snare your mind with a sense of futility, failure, endless fears, and insecurities.

Unconditional

Forgiving may feel like it lets someone off the hook. And that's too easy. Emotions beg, *Make them pay.* Evangelist John Haggai, in his book *My Son Johnny*, asked, "How do I forgive the drunk physician who stumbled into the delivery room and botched the delivery of my only child? How do I forgive someone who has never acknowledged his callous stupidity? He's ruined my son's life but, even so, I think I could forgive him if he apologized, but he ducks when he sees me. That makes me furious. The physician owes me an apology."

> Forgiving is a choice that turns survival into victorious living.

Dr. Haggai was right. The doctor owed the family an apology. Yet Dr. Haggai knew it was wrong to believe the apology would help him forgive. Forgiveness is unconditional; if a condition must be met, the act changes from forgiveness to a dutiful response. He forgave—after he grieved.[1]

A precondition never births forgiveness because it places the burden on someone else. If the person around whom we have hung the prerequisite does not meet the demand, we feel justified in our continued hurt or anger. If the prerequisites are met, we feel duty bound to abide by our promise to forgive. We say to ourselves, *Conditions are met for forgiveness, so I must get rid of the hurt or angry feelings.* The mind stuffs the emotions behind a closed door and tries to ignore them, even when they bang on the door to get out.

Not Forgetting

To forget is not the same as to forgive. The mind is a computer that stores facts. There is no erase button to expunge specific memories. Trying to forget the hurts stuffs them into the closet where each time someone or something opens

> Prerequisites destroy forgiveness.

the door, the memories jump back out, as poignant as ever. The memories tend also to seep through the cracks, oozing murky feelings that wipe out trust, prejudge performance, and make love conditional.

True forgiveness stores indiscretions and wrongs in the file under the heading "No Longer Relevant Except for Lessons." If something triggers the memory, it is remembered as a sad or difficult time, but one from which we have grown wiser. It testifies of a new beginning that sprang from hard-earned insights and a new appreciation for someone else's needs. Forgiveness allows us to grow as a result of lessons learned and prevents hardening of the heart from bitterness.

Blocked by Pride

The chief block to forgiveness is pride. I cannot count the number of times I have heard, "No way will I forgive. She does not deserve it." The stories I have heard make me want to cringe, cut off a few crucial body parts, or do a bloodletting. There is no question that many people harm others intentionally or for such purely selfish reasons that they do not *deserve* forgiveness. The mind argues, *Why should I forgive? How can I forgive when I have been so unfairly treated?* Pride cries out, *Why should I let her off the hook?* Pride fails to realize that the one on the hook is the one who doesn't let the wrong go. Pride may be justified in believing that what happened was not fair, but hanging on to it only adds to the weight of the injustice.

Crucial to Future Happiness

Who could argue that the young mother of a one-year-old, pregnant with her second child, is wrong to hate the man who left her to be free of such responsibility? How could one correct the man who rages against his son who drove their company to bankruptcy by hidden expenditures? Only an insensitive person would tell parents of a teenager who was beaten and raped, left for dead, and now survives brain-injured that they should forgive the rapist. But if any of these people hope to find happiness again, forgiveness is crucial. They become victors, no matter the tragedies they suffer, if they let go of the rage and hate and make the best of their situation. They become beacons to the rest of us struggling to make it through the storms.

Some professionals state emphatically that it is not necessary to forgive to feel better about yourself and find inner peace. They postulate that forgiveness has two requirements:

1. giving up justifiable revenge
2. absolving the guilty party of responsibility

Fulfilling either of these requirements, they state, not only is impossible but distorts the emotions. Unfortunately, if you buy into this convoluted reasoning, you will never be free of the hurts that beg you to nurture them.

Forgiveness is not about exoneration or absolution of the wrongdoer. You can't absolve someone of the wrong she did, even if that's your desire. The person who does wrong is responsible for the act. Your saying she isn't responsible does not change that fact. *Forgiveness is about the victim not being victimized two times: first by the wrong, then by a misguided requirement to hang on to the wrong.* Forgiveness is about freedom to live above the hurt and to go on with joy in your heart, in spite of the injustices.

The second fallacy in what some professionals say about forgiveness is labeling revenge "justifiable." Revenge is never justifiable. Justice, reaping the consequences of one's actions, being held responsible for what one does, these are right. Revenge, however, is a self-inflicted retaliation, the eye-for-an-eye. It's like shooting yourself in the head, to pay someone back for shooting you in the foot. Wrong never justifies wrong.

> Wrong never justifies wrong.

Forgiving Yourself

Perhaps you are the one who needs to be forgiven. It is always nice if someone you have harmed forgives you, but the person who *most* needs to forgive you is yourself. Forgiving is an inside job. It says, *I'm sorry and I won't do that again.* Most important, it says, *I will learn from my mistake.* Trying to earn forgiveness is a hopeless task. You cannot earn enough, be enough, or do enough to undo the wrong that has been done. Wrong never goes away. It just is. The only thing that turns a wrong around is when one grows from it. You can do that, with or without someone's accepting your apology, if you forgive yourself.

> Forgiving is an inside job.

We can crawl like a worm in the dirt or we can fly free, determining never to live in the mud again. My son Brad found the most beautiful four-inch-long caterpillar in our yard. It looked like the Chinese dragon paraded in the New Year's parade in New York City, lime green, great bubbles of a body, black spikes, horns, and wonderful black designs. It was so magnificent, but I wondered what incredible destruction a caterpillar of this size might have wrought. We put it in an aquarium with dirt and watched it burrow beneath the soil to wrap itself in a cocoon. It took one year before he broke free from his self-inflicted bindings. In the place of that beautiful, but destructive, caterpillar was a marvelous orange, beige, black, and red five-inch moth whose sole purpose in life would be to spread beauty. The most beautiful creatures in this world fly free from their cocoons because they unwrap their bindings. No one unwraps the bindings for them. Likewise, no one can unwrap your bindings for you.

> No one unwraps your bindings for you.

A Decision

The turning point that allows you to process out the junk that poisons your joy is simply deciding that the negative, hurting, unforgiving spirit within you is no longer acceptable. A bad start, sad years, and hard times are not the end of the world. Forgive and the hard times become growth times, the sad times make the good times more precious, and overcoming a bad start becomes a source of pride, pointing to your strength to overcome. You may ask, "How?" The answer is: Simply decide to! The feelings will follow the action. You take a journey by putting one foot in front of the other. That's how you start the process of forgiving. Decide you are going to do it and then start walking.

Forgiveness is not:

- forgetting
- absolving the person of her wrongdoing

- easier as time passes
- unrealistic
- earned
- easy

Forgiveness is:

- crucial to emotional and spiritual health
- hard work
- a way to move on and let go
- a possibility of turning hurts into growth lessons
- a gift of freedom you give to yourself and sometimes receive from another
- a choice to stop looking back

Coping with a screwed-up person is hard. It feels like a steamroller hits you at times when you try to handle the problems. It's difficult not to blow it. It feels like you are in a pressure cooker when the heat is turned up. The grandparents who were dismayed by the callousness of their daughter and aching from the loss of their grandchildren had reason to resent her hardened, noncaring, irresponsible actions. They were right to be angry just as, I am sure, you have a right to be angry at the injustices in your life. Their question to the physician was, "How many times should we forgive?" The answer is as many times as necessary to free yourself from becoming just like the person who is making you suffer.

Lifelines _____

- The primary gift of forgiveness is to free the one who forgives.

- Forgiving is a choice that turns survival into victorious living.
- Prerequisites destroy forgiveness.
- Wrong never justifies wrong.
- Forgiving is an inside job.
- No one unwraps your bindings for you.

14

How Many Times Do I Say "Sorry"?

The two most important phrases in the English language are "I'm sorry" and "I care!"

It's hard to apologize to someone who keeps your family's life in chaos, drives you crazy, or is a general pain in the neck. It seems wrong, like you are admitting that he may be right, like you blew it, like you are a part of the problem when you wouldn't be if he weren't so obnoxious. No way! Apologizing feels like groveling, and you don't want to do that! Add to the mix the fact that sometimes in the past, apologies have turned around to bash you in the head. You reason that perhaps it is better to let the wrong just go away. Won't time take care of it anyway? Actually, no! People don't forget a wrong just because you ignore it. Nor does time erase the need to say "I'm sorry!"

To apologize is to accept responsibility for something you did wrong. It is personal accountability. This demands maturity and may not be understood by others. It isn't a way to get out of something or a way to show off your humility. It isn't a kite to fly in the other person's face, followed by a tagalong tail of stipulations, conditions, or justifications. Nor is it like popcorn, coming fast, often, and from everywhere. Popcorn apologies are merely a string of words, not heartfelt assumptions of responsibility.

> An apology frees the person who offers it.

A sincere apology frees you from cowering as you accept responsibility for your own act, learn from it, and put it behind you. The past no longer sits beside you on the judgment bench. Apologizing, like forgiveness, is an inside job that not only offers release to the one who has been harmed, but frees the one who apologizes. An apology clears the air unless it is done insincerely in an effort to shift blame or relieve guilt. An apology that is made simply to manipulate others can damage and destroy.

A healthy apology must flow from inside the one who apologizes. It has three objectives:

1. Acknowledge responsibility for the wrong (I did it).
2. Assert accountability (I should not have done it).
3. Free the person who apologizes from guilt so that lessons can be gleaned from the wrong (I have learned).

Sincere apologies are not forced, are not simply an emotional display, and are the product of a determination to act with the maturity of an adult. President Clinton will be held up forever as a great example of a failed apology. He invalidated his apology for lying and marital infidelity when he apologized but tagged on to it finger-pointing at independent counsel Kenneth Starr. Watching him apologize was like watching a child, "I did it, but you made me." He did wrong and needed to simply admit it. He could have said, "I did wrong. I'm sorry. I shouldn't have lied. I'm sorry for all the people I have hurt—my family, Monica Lewinsky and her family, and you who have believed my cover-up. I was wrong."

People knew why he lied. No one wants to be caught with a hand in the cookie jar or, in this case, with his pants down. For months the news media spun off his bad apology, suggesting it should be done again. The world shrugged. An apology that is forced is accepted for what it is—nothing but words without meaning. Clinton's apologies left no doubt that he was genuinely sorry—sorry that he got caught.

Steps in an Apology

An effective apology is like the five fingers on a hand. The fingers represent location, timing, preparation, focus, and presentation. For the hand to work properly, the fingers must work together. Here are some important things that set the stage for a successful apology.

Location

Choose a neutral location, one that does not make either person feel uncomfortable or overpowered. Choose a place where there will be as little distraction as possible from telephone calls, children, or people who can overhear. No others should be present, unless your wrong requires a broader acknowledgment. For instance, if you have made a false accusation or have publicly humiliated someone, you need to apologize to the person and also make a public correction. It is wise to apologize to the individual first and ask his or her permission to correct it publicly.

Timing

In general, the sooner you apologize the better. The old saying "Never let the sun go down on your anger" is a wise injunction. Simmering anger grows exponentially as time drags it out. However, don't rush the apology. Recognize and appreciate the person's cooldown style. Some people can hear an apology seconds after the wrong has been committed, but others need time to cool down. When you do apologize, be sure there will be plenty of time to talk out the issues. Listen, but do not allow the session to degenerate into an attack session.

Preparation

Practice what you are going to say. Keep in mind that effective apologies flow from caring, not perfection. Organizing your thoughts on paper may help you narrow and define the apology. Think through what you want to say and how you will word the apology to accept responsibility for specific acts without attempting to justify the wrong. Simple is best.

Sometimes it may be helpful to write out the apology so that you are certain it contains the six specific components that should be embodied in an apology: (1) preliminary conversation, (2) acknowledgment of the specific wrong, (3) acknowledgment of the hurt that was caused, (4) a plan for making amends, (5) a plan for future behavior, and (6) the lesson you learned.

Focus

Stay focused on the goal—to say "I'm sorry" for what you did wrong. Be careful not to focus on the incident that initiated your unacceptable response. If you were angry, you may be able to keep your anger in check by thinking of things you appreciate about the person.

Presentation

An apology should be simple and to the point as it puts concern for someone else in front of self-gain or self-protection. Your caring will be evident in your words, inflections, gestures, and reactions. When you approach the person you have offended, be calm and pleasant. Make small talk for a few moments to ease the tension. Then get to the point and be specific with your apology.

For example, let's pretend you said something that later you realized was hurtful. An apology containing the six essential components could be: "Thank you for meeting with me. I want to apologize for. . . . I did not mean to hurt your feelings. I want to make amends by giving you this flower. I picked it thinking of how special you are to me. I will not be such a jerk in the future. I learned it is best to get the whole story before I jump in."

Be cautious. Wait out interruptions. Accept full responsibility for your part in the wrong and offer no justifications. Express hope for a better, stronger relationship. Leave if the session turns sour.

Don't use "all" or "never" words tagged to your "I'm sorry":

We never get along.
We always fight.

You always . . .
I never feel like . . .

Always leave room for hope to follow the apology:

I feel sure we will do better.
I hope you know how much I care.
I know we can make this work.

Inappropriate Apologies

Probably everyone of us has experienced a disingenuous apology—one that was forced, insincere, or cutting. The insincerity of an apology is very hard to disguise. So if you are going to apologize, make it sincere. It's true that humbling yourself enough to apologize is much more difficult than sweeping the problem under the rug, but if you are going to stand as an adult, overcome the inner voice that begs to justify your wrong. And don't apologize simply out of obligation. This apology simply appeases the one hurt (if he doesn't see through its insincerity), but it doesn't free the one who did the wrong.

Some apologies are inappropriate. *It is inappropriate to apologize for taking a stand against evil or wrongs.* Anger is justified when the boundaries of safety, decency, and respect are trampled. In fact, at such times to not be hurt or angry is a symptom of mental, emotional, or spiritual disorder. When you observe evil or wrong, you may overreact and lose control. You can be sorry for that and express your intention to never lose control again, but that assumes that the other person understands and respects the boundaries: I apologized for losing my cool with my boss, but I finally told him I could not work overtime anymore this month. . . . It would be stupid to lose my marriage because I have a workaholic boss. . . . I am sorry I yelled, but I will not allow you to hit my child or verbally cut her to pieces. Correcting her is my job.

Don't apologize for wrong thoughts. Charles Stanley tells the story of a young man who asked a woman on his staff to forgive him for lusting after her. She was shocked and felt embarrassed and self-conscious around him from then on. Maybe he thought he was actually flirting or trying to flatter the woman, but in reality, he was tactless.

False humility is inappropriate. Some people apologize, apologize, apologize. It may be because they want what can never be—an erased past. Or people who apologize repeatedly may have nothing for which to apologize but they like the image of humility.

An apology should not be self-flagellation, proof that you are unworthy, a failure, and inadequate. My husband received a letter from a medical school colleague who had become convicted by his guilt. In medical school he had stolen another student's microscope. Twenty years later this man was seeking absolution, so he wrote everyone in his medical school class begging for forgiveness. He did not suggest he would return the microscope or pay for it if the owner identified himself. He was just flogging himself, beating himself up, which does no one any good. He was seeking approval and affirmation, as he attempted to use the apology to clear his inside problem. Blanket apologies are given by someone on a penance journey who has filed wrongs too long under "Guilty." Such apologies flow from belly button focus. The individual is looking down instead of freeing himself by looking up.

If, like the physician, you don't know whom you have harmed, consider carefully the wisdom of your approach to apologizing. When a physician is treating a patient, he wouldn't load the patient up with every medicine in the cabinet. He would do the footwork necessary to discover the right drug for the specific need. Perhaps in our personal arena we need to follow the same approach—when there is doubt, narrow the field to find the right target for an apology.

Confession

Confession is sharing an indiscretion with someone who does not know of your guilt. It is done to seek absolution, clear the air, or seek someone's okay to wipe the slate clean. Confession may be good for you but may not be good for the one to whom you confess. Certainly it is good to address buried transgressions, but you must consider carefully to whom you confess. A professional counselor or priest/minister/rabbi are good choices. But too often a confession is made to the "victim" whose self-esteem is blown out of the water by the bombshell. I wonder if the confession is a subconscious attempt to put the onus of guilt on the victim, to sweep the junk onto someone else's doorstep.

On the national television program *Sixty Minutes*, Bill McCartney, the founder of Promise Keepers, and his wife were asked about the marital infidelity he had publicly acknowledged. Years before on a road trip with his football team, he had had a one-night stand. His marriage after this public confession lay in shambles; his wife attempted suicide; he was on a treadmill trying to make up for his wrong. Did his confession clear the air and lay the groundwork for a new beginning? Or did it injure an already fragile relationship beyond repair? As I watched both of them avoid eye contact, wring their hands, and stammer, it was obvious their emotions, already frayed by layers of problems, had been dealt a crushing blow.

Perhaps those planning such a confession should consider whether revelations of unknown or unsuspected transgressions of the past would be better released to someone who will not feel knifed in the back or kicked in the stomach by the information. It's not the person who has been unknowingly injured who must free the other from guilt. Guilt is an inside alarm that signals the need to change course. Once a person determines to change, he or she can look back on the past and learn from it.

> Guilt is an inside alarm that signals the need to change course.

A good general rule for a confession is simple: Confess if it will help the other person and strengthen the relationship. Use discernment if the confession will simply relieve your guilt but bring anguish to the other person. Certainly we want to be honest in our relationships, but we must be careful not to use a tell-all session as a search for absolution.

Repeat Apologies

If the record is stuck, pick up the needle. If you have apologized, be content. Past wrongs offer you two options: (1) Use them as a learning tool for the present, or (2) use them as an excuse to fail. "I blew it, so I'll never be the person I should be." That's a cop-out. Perhaps you keep apologizing because you like feeling beaten down or you are hooked in a behavior for which you need outside help. There are a lot of alcoholics who are teetotalers, kleptomaniacs who no longer steal, cheaters who have stopped cheating, abusers who have stopped abusing because they sought and accepted outside help. If you are really sorry and intend to change, only one apology for your wrong is necessary!

When an Apology Is Refused

Sometimes an apology is refused. The person you apologize to says, "You are too late . . . too wrong . . . not sincere enough . . . have not done enough penance." Bear in mind: An apology is made by the one who accepts responsibility for his wrong action and offers the one wronged the opportunity to let the wrong be forgotten. The refusal may sting and bury you in deep regret, but the reality is that it's up to the other person. If he does not intend to forgive, you must move on, refusing to snivel. If you wallow and grovel, chains of remorse and guilt will bind you. Difficult relationships often spin off this type of interaction where one dominates the whimpering, repentant soul. No healthy relationship survives when one person scrapes along on his knees while the other stands over her. Sincere apologies are freeing. Don't let the other person's reaction take your freedom away.

When You Can't Apologize

Sometimes an apology face-to-face, written, or by phone is not possible. Death, health problems, politics of the situation, moves, and even resistance may not allow it. Viktor Frankl in *Man's Search for Meaning* addressed the guilt that overwhelmed survivors of the Nazi concentration camps.[1] They knew, regardless of any good they had done, that their personal survival had depended on being selfish and self-centered, of hoarding the last crumb of bread, a blanket, and shoes. They remembered standing by as friends were humiliated and tortured. It was too late to undo or apologize for wrongs. They had been freed by the Allies from their prisons, but *inside* they were still captive.

You may not be able to apologize. It may be too late for someone to apologize to you. From the horrific guilt of the concentration camps, psychiatrist Viktor Frankl affirms spiritual truth: It is not the act of apologizing or being apologized to that frees us from guilt; it is where we focus, on the guilt or the lessons, on the past or the present. No one can change his or her past experiences, but each of us can change our present by seeing the past mistakes, hurts, and injustices as just what they are, the past. Apologize to yourself that you did something wrong or that you clung to someone else's hurts and wasted your precious time, if you can't apologize directly to the person. Say to yourself, "I'm sorry I blew it. I'm sorry I wasted a precious opportunity. I'm sorry I hurt someone. I will use that failure to learn better ways to handle present difficulties."

> An apology begins the first day of the rest of your life.

Perhaps it would be helpful to write a letter to the person, even though you know it cannot be delivered. Write out your thoughts, your regret, and what you are going to do with the lesson. Thank the person for being the catalyst for your growth. Perhaps, if the lesson you learned was significant, you will want to share the insight with a loved one of the person to whom you are apologizing. Sharing how you got the insight is not necessary but, rather, how the other person helped you grow significantly, how his life touched yours.

Frankl's experience taught him a new basis for moving on from the past—recognition that today is a first day, the first day of the rest of one's life. Give yourself a first day. First days don't require that you have it all figured out; they just require your conscious decision to overpower the internal voices that want to pull you down and lock you into the past.

Apologize if you can. If it's not possible, learn the lessons. Move on. This is the first day of the rest of your life.

Lifelines

- An apology frees the person who offers it.
- Guilt is an inside alarm that signals the need to change course.
- An apology begins the first day of the rest of your life.

Touch with Words

Heartfelt communication begins with a handshake.

It is impossible to talk with someone who twists words, won't listen, misinterprets, and stands staunchly in her position, regardless of the facts that support a different conclusion. So what do you do if you are in a relationship in which presentation of your ideas, goals, or needs hits a wall? Do you give up and just keep your opinions to yourself, or do you yell louder? How is it possible to communicate with someone who knows it all, intends to stay ahead of everyone else on practically every issue, and desires for you to do her bidding without any hope of hearing your needs? How do you live with the inevitable stress without ruining your health or becoming screwed up yourself? Is it possible to touch with words, or is

177

that an idealistic dream that works in normal relationships but not with people who are intently self-focused and self-enthroned? How do you get through the layers of miscommunication that swirl in difficult relationships when you are on different wavelengths?

The Art of Communication

In life we don't necessarily get what we deserve. It is often because our own efforts get in the way. Nothing is truer for difficult relationships—our own words cause us to choke. We get so hung up on trying to be heard, wanting to get our point across, correcting the ridiculous, or changing the off-the-wall commentary that we stick our foot in our mouth and chew on it.

If you are dealing with screwed-up people, it may help you to understand:

They do not hear.

They will not listen.

You cannot change them by trying to change them.

They will not follow your logic.

They believe what they want to believe.

So how do you communicate? If communication is a hand-shake, a negotiation, how is it possible with such a person? It isn't! Not in the usual sense of one person sharing his ideas with another to bring about a compromise solution, each hoping to broaden understandings and find a peaceful resolution. Communication with most people is an art, but with difficult people it is an understanding that regardless of what you say, you may not be heard.

Building and maintaining the best possible relationship, especially with a difficult person, depends on your understanding the way in which your words and their delivery will affect the person to whom you are speaking. Words are precious tools that require skilled implementation. Depending on how they are put together and the tone of voice used, words are able to touch, encourage, hug, push away, and/or bash. They are gifts of concern, caring, and encouragement, or they are weapons of rebuke, criticism, and rejection. They can, with one phrase, forgive and soon after be a sledgehammer of suspicion, probing questions, and ingratiating comments. Too often when we are coping with a difficult person, our words become wedges, splitting open wounds and axing hope as they pound or cut.

Books are written on how to communicate effectively with those who are willing to listen, but it helps to go a bit deeper when we address effective communication with people who are not there to negotiate and shake hands. We need ways to make peace with the fact that we may never be heard, may always find the conversations lead to war games, and may be overwhelmed by the air of superiority—or incredible need— underlying the communication. Even so, keep in mind that difficult people read us clearly. They hear the caring or the disgust. Smiles do not hide negative feelings. They stiffen against criticism lurking behind begrudged agreement.

Kind words touch every heart. In Boston my husband and I lived next door to a newcomer to America. He spoke English enough to get to work, buy his groceries, and get home, but our attempts to communicate to him the basics of community life, such as how garbage is picked up, were a challenge. Still he heard our caring through the tone of our jumbled words, read it in our gestures, and felt it in his heart. Isn't that what you want with the person in your life who creates such chaos? You stay in the relationship because you care and you want to communicate the caring, even as you find ways to live in peace with the challenges that make your life with the person less than ideal.

The How-Tos of Communication

Laugh about the miscommunication as much as you can. See the humor in it as we did with our Bostonian friend. Don't laugh *at* your SUP. Laugh *with* her. Shake your head—not in anger, but with laughter. Say, "I surely would never have thought of it this way! . . . Are you sure? . . . How did you come to those conclusions?" Laughter keeps the fists from forming. Laughter allows you to be objective, to have that aerial perspective.

Combine kind acts with words. I like to remember Senator Harold Hughes, who was to speak to the five hundred guests in attendance at the national prayer breakfast in Washington, D.C., when a waitress dropped a tray of desserts on him. Amidst a flurry of apologies and hushed silence as stunned bystanders watched, the chagrined waitress tried to wipe the gooey mess off the senator's coat and white shirt.

The senator's murmuring, "It's okay. It's all right," did not wipe the look of pain from the waitress's face. When the last bit of cherry cobbler was cleaned up, the woman gathered her towels to go. Senator Hughes saw that her pain and embarrassment were evident. He knew his words had not been absorbed, even though they were sincere. So the senator stood, touched her still red face, and gently kissed her cheek. The blush disappeared, and in its place a smile spread over her face. She left the room, radiant, head erect, and without shame. Instead of an act that would be remembered with disgrace, this young woman would retell her story remembering that "Senator Harold Hughes kissed me right there in front of all those people after I had just dropped cherry cobbler all over him!"

Senator Hughes understood how words can help or harm. He knew that sometimes, no matter how well the words are communicated, they are not heard. He understood that when gentle words are followed by acts of kindness, the words are heard through walls of anger, guilt, shame, or pain.[1]

Begin with the end in mind. Focus on the goal so that you do not get sidetracked in defensive reactions. This is one of the hab-

> Communication is a combination of right words and sensitive acts.

its of highly effective people. If our automatic pilot locks up on the past, the unfairness, or any other impediment, our emotions take over, demanding answers: Why are you letting her get away with that remark? . . . Don't you care that she isn't listening? . . . What's wrong with her that she can't get the story straight?

A woman sobbed as she told me her story. Her two sons had died. Her first son, "the good son" as she described him, had contracted the hepatitis virus his junior year in medical school and died from its complications. Grief overwhelmed her.

A year later her younger son did something that infuriated her. Perhaps he had stolen money from her pocketbook. Maybe he was on drugs, drunk, not being responsible. Difficult relationships can drive us crazy. She yelled at him, "It should have been you!" He paused, looked at his mother, and, as he left, said, "I know. It should have been me."

Three hours later a policeman came to her door. "I'm sorry," he said. "We found your son. He shot himself in the head."

The woman was on automatic pilot when her thoughtless words slipped out. "If only I had focused on how grateful I was to still have my son," she cried.

Problems, emotions, and screwed-up behavior can put you on automatic pilot and destroy the chance for reconciliation or for just developing a more normal relationship. Surely you don't want to look back and see lost opportunities to reach out in love and perhaps bring about change.

Be bigger than a screwed-up person if you want to communicate effectively with her. When she is stepping on your toes, don't let pride obscure your goal. You have to keep your head on straight when your words are twisted, your efforts denigrated, or there is little response at all. You can't be sensitive when she hangs up on you or slams the door in your face. You have to remember love and caring and your commitment to the relationship. Comfort yourself with the knowledge that you are acting more maturely, regardless of age.

Touch with words. Often the best way to respond to someone difficult is with a caress. A baby communicates with garbled language and yet he is understood. Even his hands talk. If he stretches out his hand, the baby is asking for something. If he reaches up gently and caresses your face between his hands, he is saying, "I love you." Isn't touching with words what you want? You want the person with whom you are having difficulty communicating to hear you, even if she can't accept your words. You want the caring to show through, even if the goals and agendas are divergent. Your demeanor is crucial to communication.

Develop a duck's back attitude. Begin by treating the difficult person with as much respect as you do other acquaintances or the eccentric at your workplace. Let the negatives bounce off like water off a duck's back. Ingest the good; reject the bad. What does it matter? Let the SUP haggle, carry on, scream, or preach. She is behaving that way to be seen and accepted. It's laughable. It's sad.

Keep your mouth shut. Turning off the difficult person after she gets started is like turning off the rain. So you might as well not try. Keep your mouth shut, keep your cool, and wait until she's finished. If you try to interrupt or refute her arguments, you may encourage her to continue her harangue even longer. Wait it out without being drawn into an argument.

Listen without being bullish. We have a tendency to turn off difficult people. They talk so much that you assume everything they say is unbalanced. You may be right. What they say may make no sense, but it's to your advantage to listen. It isn't the person who corrects someone else's misstatements or choices that is smart; rather, it is the person who offers that individual options that save her dignity. This is the kind thing to do and will keep you from being reactive. Listen and then do your homework before trying to dissuade your SUP from her point of view. This will keep you out of unnecessary conflict that will build more walls. An "umm, I'll check this out" attitude is crucial to communication.

A difficult patient in a nursing home assured my husband that a medicine the nurses were giving her was making her sleepy. Paul reviewed the medical chart with this woman, talking to her about each medicine. He knew the medications on the chart had no drowsiness side effect. The patient agreed but stood her ground. "I know none of those medicines make me sleepy, but the nurses are giving me something that does," she said.

Rather than argue with the elderly patient, Paul took her with him to the nurses' station. He showed the chart to the nurse and asked her to review it against her chart. Sure enough, there was a tranquilizer on the nurse's chart that was a carryover from a hospitalization weeks before. The patient was right. Fortunately Paul did not have to retract his statements or apologize for his actions, because his respect for the woman kept him from countering her assertions. It's the same when we deal with screwed-up people. Keeping the options open and not jumping to conclusions will prevent chaos from erupting. Off-the-wall people get louder and stronger the more they are not heard. You may not like the person. You may not believe her complaints, explanations, or positions, but when you respect her right to her opinions, it keeps the noise down.

I have found that many of the people we find difficult in our life have superb creative ideas. They simply are lacking in communication skills. Or they are stuck in one area, perhaps with just one person. The presentation of their ideas is often rejected because of the strong—or wimpy—way they impart them, so they end up screaming all the louder or hiding in their shell like a turtle.

Be an echo. Echo back in the form of statements what is being said. You may say such things as: I feel your concern about . . . You are saying that . . . I appreciate your delving into this so deeply to find . . . Listen without rancor. Your attitude will show if you are busy coming up with a defense or thinking how ridiculous she is, rather than trying to hear and repeat.

It is hard to argue with an echo, and, amazingly, when a person hears her own words echoed back, quite often one of three things happens: (1) she decides it doesn't sound quite right and so begins to be more open to other ideas; (2) she quits being so defensive because she finds someone is listening; or (3) possibly, as in my husband's case, the person's words are verified.

Echoing back what you hear is important for these reasons:

1. You show that you are listening.
2. Your perceived respect will open the door for you to express some thoughts—perhaps!
3. Misinterpreted statements can be corrected.
4. Options may be explored.
5. It keeps blame games from being played.
6. Listening and echoing encourage compromise.
7. It keeps down the friction and wall-building.
8. You are able to be less emotionally involved.

A man in a seminar discussion group shared his experience: "I remember the first time I successfully listened to the difficult person in my life, listened without thinking in my mind: *Wrong . . . Here we go again . . . Can't believe she said that . . . Inconceivable!* I just listened as if this person in my life was someone I wanted to know, understand, and respect. I didn't try to correct the misstatements and crazy thoughts, didn't demean, put down, criticize, or hurl back inflammatory statements. It was exhilarating. And, you know, the remarkable thing is I actually enjoyed the conversation."

What this man did was not easy. It was probably all he could do to keep from rolling his eyes, defending himself or others, or snapping back. He listened—not just to the words, but also to the needs and to the underlying drives. He began to hear what he had never heard before: The person talking to him was someone who desperately needed his attention, someone who was talking with such authority because she didn't feel appreciated or heard. When someone always has to be right, superior, critical, whiny, or hostile, she is on the defensive. Compassion flows from listening with your heart as well as your ears.

Another way to echo is with questions. A lot of conflict can be skirted by simply echoing back in the form of a question the statements that are blustering forth: Are you saying . . . ? Did I understand correctly . . . ? Is your understanding that . . . ? From your personal experience have you found what you are saying to be true?

Begin with the end in mind.

Praise. Many a hardened soul has softened by simple praise. You don't have to lie. You don't have to uphold the view or opinion. Use neutral words and comments to keep the other person from becoming defensive about your praise. It should be appropriate, such as: You are so enthusiastic about what you believe . . . I wish I had some of your zeal! . . . You are so good at projecting what you think . . . Here are some other good phrases to use:

- I had not thought of it in that light.
- Really? How interesting.
- That's something new.
- You may be right.
- Umm. You've studied this a lot.
- Incredible! I never would have connected that . . .
- It's good you are investigating the options.
- You've searched for the answers. Are you comfortable with the advice you've received?

Nothing feels better than being in control when you talk with someone you have been unable to communicate successfully with for years—if ever. Let's reiterate the ways to communicate with difficult people without becoming defensive: Have a sense of humor about miscommunication. Combine kind acts with words. Begin with the end in mind.

Keep your pride from taking over. Use words to touch. Don't take offenses seriously. Keep your mouth shut and listen. Echo, using statements and questions. Praise.

Even when you know what to do, you will still be challenged. Screwed-up people are not a reasonable lot. You may do well, then tire and sense the anxiety rising. If you feel you are losing control and must correct or challenge, excuse yourself. Sometimes little doses are all you can handle, even with the end in mind.

Don't Fight Their Battles

You don't have to fight a difficult person's battles. You don't have to defend her actions. What she does, even if it affects you, is her problem. However, separating yourself from the actions of someone who is part of you—a child, parent, spouse, sibling, relative, close friend—is painful. It leaves a hole in your soul. You will grieve for the lost dreams, the lost potential, the lost relationship. But if you want to be emotionally healthy and find peace within your circumstances, separation is critical.

The urge to explain, to defend, to support, regardless of the behavior, is urgent when you are connected or feel responsible. Don't do it unless the balance is terribly one-sided, as in the protection of children. Those who have little ability to discern the wrong or truth of the situation need guidance so they are not overcome by it.

"I know what it is to want to crawl out through the crack in the floor," said my grocer. "I invited my brother to hear a speaker at my club. After the meeting in front of my friends, he proceeds to verbally pummel the man. The speaker was shocked. My inclination was to jump in and defend my brother. Then I wanted to defend the speaker.

Finally, I walked away. The speaker was an adult. He could handle his own battles. He would learn another skill from the experience of being verbally slugged by a person in his audience!"

Other situations demand your help, but to help means taking your ego out of the picture. Your help will probably not be appreciated. For instance, your elderly, fiercely independent, difficult father becomes addicted to drugs after your mother's death. His denial, his refusal to accept your help, and his deep need may cause him to lash out at you more strongly than ever. Regardless, you do what you must do, including such things as spending more time with him, limiting his driving, and talking honestly about the problem. You may need to call the physicians who are giving out the medication for support in limiting the pills. Do what you can.

Winning Isn't Crucial

Winning isn't the goal of healthy communication. Being right isn't the most important thing. If you or someone else is being misrepresented, however, correct the misunderstanding. Say,

- Sorry, but you misunderstood what I was saying.
- I do not believe (someone's name) feels that way.
- That is not my understanding.

Avoid debate or battle or even restating the point again and again. Be simple, direct, and speak without rancor.

A nurse shared that a patient emphatically and incorrectly stated her health problem. The nurse corrected her several times and then shut her mouth. The patient obviously did not choose to hear and clung to her version of the truth. Continuing to try to change or impress the woman with the facts would merely have created a barrier.

Stephen Covey suggests in *The Seven Habits of Highly Effective People* that successful communication provides a win-win opportunity.[2] To make communication a win-win implies we first listen to understand and then share our thoughts as we work toward compromise and resolution. With difficult people a third step must come into play— reality. Unity within diversity may be the goal. You may hope for working together, joining forces, becoming part- ners, but, too often, that isn't real. Remember, compromise implies a handshake with a promise to come together to agree. Unfortunately, in difficult relationships at least one person has her own agenda that precludes compromise. That agenda is expressed in "I can do it myself!" and "I want my way!"

C. Everett Koop, surgeon general of the United States from 1968 to 1977, was strongly opposed to abortion, but when Congress asked him to write the third draft of a bill that could appease both the pro-choice and pro-life proponents who were unable to compromise on the first two drafts, he agreed. He knew that the pro-life group would never accept unfettered access to abortion, and he knew the pro-choice group would oppose a platform that denied abortion on any grounds. So he drafted a bill that allowed abortion on four grounds: rape, incest, the life of the mother, and horrific birth deformities.

The pro-life proponents refused to budge from their stance, so the bill was defeated. Koop, though personally opposed to abortion on any grounds, stood behind the bill. He observed sadly, "If compromise could have been reached, though it was not what either group ultimately wanted, only

5 percent of the current three million per year abortions would have taken place."[3]

Ask yourself: What might I compromise that could save a good part of my dreams and communicate my willingness to try to work through my problems in my difficult relationship? Figure out what is possible. The goal of good communication is unity within diversity. In a difficult relationship, however, communication is also about survival.

Do What You Must Do

Twisted entanglements in relationships are powerful drivers of the emotions. You may want to be nice, but your communication ends up sounding like a cry of despair rather than words of encouragement. You feel like the screwed-up person in your life has you in a vice that is getting tighter and tighter. How are you supposed to be distanced from a person who is bound to you by deeply ingrained needs? You feel desperate to communicate what you want, think, and need. Your emotions are frayed hot wires.

> The goal of good communication is unity within diversity.

Perhaps the twisting is around finances, love, children. Your ex-wife (or in-law) threatens you with withdrawal of your visitation rights to your children (or the grandchildren). Maybe you are responsible for small children, have no commercial skills, and feel captive to the man who likes his sex but treats you like an enemy. Is your boss horrid, but you are desperate for the job? What if your twisted business partner holds the keys to your financial survival? It may be that an adult child is nearly causing your bankruptcy or is locked in a marriage where physical abuse threatens her life.

Figure out what is possible—and move on. No question, the likelihood of the ideal resolution to your problem is slim. Yet it's guaranteed that tactics such as screaming, yelling, fighting, battling, arguing, and/or pleading will set your SUP's twisted behavior into concrete as it ties you in knots. Be a realist. The problem is highly unlikely to resolve itself or go away. The only thing that brings a screw out of the board it has been screwed into is a decision, a plan of action, and a lot of work. Do what you must do, even as you try your best to work with the problem person. Sometimes the best resolution is that you agree to disagree. Whatever you do, remember:

The way I say something is as important as what I say.

I am responsible for my words and acts.

I must be open about my thoughts and feelings.

I will be sensitive to the underlying need of the difficult person in my life—the need to be heard and appreciated.

I will do right, regardless of what is done to me.

I will be objective and as distanced from the chaos as possible.

I will validate the person with whom I am conversing by taking seriously what she says, though I will use common sense and experience in accepting its validity.

I will develop a plan of action based on the reality of what is possible.

Harmonious communication and compromise are goals that will improve your relationship with your SUP. But, with a difficult person, communication may feel like sticking your neck out for the ax to fall. But behold the turtle. He makes progress only when he sticks his neck out.

Lifelines

- Communication is a combination of right words and sensitive acts.
- Begin with the end in mind.
- The goal of good communication is unity within diversity.

16

Is "Different" Screwed Up?

The moon and oceans create tides—two uniquely different forces working together.

Throughout nature we see that productive relationships are forged by the union of uniquely different forces—the moon and the oceans create tides, electrons and neutrons create electricity, acids work with alkaline for digestion, fine co-ordination is the product of two opposing muscle groups, the sun and moon light the day and night. Different is good. Yet, though we affirm those differences and acknowledge their reality in nature, we tend to demand conformity when it comes to how people around us live their lives.

Different is fine as long as it doesn't invade our inner circle or come too close to how we live. That's why all of us understand the whispered innuendo about the outsider by marriage—he (or she) is not one of the family. We can identify with the pride a parent feels when someone comments about his or her child, "Why, he's just like you." If "different" is a member of the family, he is kept on the fringe, not a full-fledged member. That person is considered messed up, hard to get along with, out-to-lunch, embarrassing, or a pain. How sad! Different can

- enrich
- broaden
- increase the possibilities

Mark I. Rosen writes, "We admire traits in others that we admire in ourselves; we denigrate others when their behavior doesn't conform to our values. We find it almost impossible to climb inside someone else's head and see the world through different eyes."[1]

So what should we do when those close to us are *different* and those differences drive us crazy? The governor didn't know what to do. A multimillionaire, founder of a large energy-engineering firm, he was elected by a landslide vote to the governorship of his state. He excelled as a motivator, leader, and strong negotiator. His generosity and good works were exemplary. He knew how to get things done, he knew how to find solutions, and he knew how to set goals for the future. He knew how to handle the world, but he was at a loss when it came to his family.

The governor worked beautifully with people outside his close circles. He allowed for differences, patting them on the back, encouraging them along, cheering their progress. His inner circle of business and political friends were like him—aggressive, charming, and winners. He was stimulated by their different approaches to work, which enlightened him to new possibilities. But at home in the intimate circle, he saw *different* as threatening. He couldn't understand why his wife and son didn't have the same drive and ambition he did. He was puzzled by his wife, who preferred to stay home to standing by his side in public.

> Different doesn't have to be wrong.

It rankled him that his only son, who could find limitless opportunities because of his father's position, wanted to be left alone to listen to his music and log on to the Internet.

He wondered why strangers idolized him, close friends applauded him, yet his own family seemed unimpressed with the advantages he made available to them. He found dealing with his wife and son exhausting. He didn't realize that he perceived them, not as they were but as he wanted them to be, and they missed the mark.

From the wife and son's point of view, it was the governor who was *different*. The wife wondered what was wrong with him. "My husband is a saint at work but a barbarian at home. He gives out lists of dos in the morning and checks them off at night. He lines us up and fires his guns, his 'you shoulds.' I don't know why he refuses to see the good we do."

And his son was angry. "Dad's a pusher. He's all laughs outside, but he's the pits at home." Differences can drive people apart if they engender criticism rather than appreciation.

Reality Checks

I find reality checks helpful to stop my criticizing what is different within my intimate and close circles. They balance my thoughts and emotions so that I can determine whether an approach, expression, or view is wrong and potentially hurtful or just *different* from mine. It keeps me from seeing different as threatening or a personal attack. It helps me appreciate *different* as a way to expand my horizons and not an obstacle in my course. Wrong behavior needs to be recognized and, if possible, changed. Different simply needs to be acknowledged and appreciated. We shouldn't try to change someone just because he is different. If we do, we may be tampering with his basic nature, and we may not be pleased with the consequences:

We may destroy the person's self-esteem.

We may kill our relationship.

We may lose the opportunity of learning to love someone for who he is rather than for who we imagine the person to be.

We may miss the opportunity to glean wisdom and breadth from his different vision.

Reality Check One: Basic Assumptions Differ

When encountering someone's perplexing behavior, it may be helpful to consider the possibility that he was taught different basic assumptions about appropriate behavior. What may seem obvious to you may not be so obvious to someone else. People can be clueless as to what you are expecting if they did not learn the same basics you did.

For example, some families take it for granted that they will telephone each other every day. Others call when something important happens. Count on hurt feelings if someone from family one marries into family two and assumes the behavior he grew up with is right and the other way wrong.

This type of "little issue" becomes the crisis that creates problems in many relationships. When these little things are compounded in an individual, he is considered *different*. It's important to discuss the issues and the basic assumptions, rather than seethe about differences. Helping someone understand what might help the interaction is better than assuming what he does is an intentional insult.

Reality Check Two: It Isn't Necessarily about Me

The past very often pokes its head into the present. More often than not, unresolved problems of the past are time bombs that tend to explode in adult relationships. Someone stuck in the past relates to you as if measuring you against someone else or responding to you as he learned to respond to someone earlier in life.

I taught school for a number of years. One of my fellow teachers was called a Snow Queen. (Remember the Hans Christian Anderson fairy tale of the beautiful Snow Queen, the most beautiful of all queens. With one glance you were captured by her beauty, but the closer you came to her, the more she chilled you.) Likewise, my coworker was a beauty, but the closer you got to her, the more you felt her controlling and critical spirit. At first I wondered what I had done. I thought long and hard to discern if I were the problem, but it became apparent that this teacher had difficulty relating to any female. She had transferred the childhood negative relationship with her mother into her adulthood relationships with women.

Recognizing that it wasn't about me freed me to shrug off the negatives and go on about my business. It was her problem, not mine. It's important to remember that when someone is difficult, it isn't necessarily because he has a problem with you.

Reality Check Three: The Effects of Personality

A person's personality has great impact on the way he or she thinks, speaks, and makes decisions about life.

Your own personality means that you appreciate some ways of behaving more than others. For example, the way someone expresses concern for you is influenced by his personality. And how you receive the comment is influenced by yours. Which of these four phrases, representing different personality types, would you understand best to be an expression of concern for you?

1. You're doing a fine job. I'm sure you'll choose wisely.
2. Call me when you get the problem worked out and we will go out to lunch.
3. You should do it like this . . .
4. I'll help you work this out.

Your choice is influenced by your personality. The comment that you would appreciate may reveal to someone else a lack of concern or, on the other side, may be considered meddling or controlling.

Personality also affects whether we need to be with people or by ourselves. Just as our physical body requires energy, emotions require energy. We feed our body food. If we are extroverts, we feed our emotions by being with people. If we are introverts, we reenergize by being alone, separated from others. The label has nothing to do with the way people act when they are together. An introvert may be charming, outgoing, and the life of the party. An extrovert may be quiet, reserved, and hesitant to share his opinion. The key to an extrovert or an introvert is what rejuvenates them. Extroverts need social interactions or they become depressed. Too much time alone sends their emotions spiraling downward. Introverts overdose on too much social time. They need to withdraw, to pull back, to have quiet time to revitalize. Without energizing as they must, both introverts and extroverts will feel dejected, question their abilities and their life purpose, and show signs of depression.

Closely related to personality is the way people draw conclusions and make decisions. People are either thinkers or feelers. People who come to decisions on the basis of logic do not understand people who go against reason to determine a course of action. Feelers think those who must follow a logical process are cold and insensitive. Feelers need thinkers; thinkers need feelers, but too often they battle each other rather than appreciating the differing perspective that offers expanded insight.

Intrinsic personality traits must be appreciated to unite diversity. I have learned to stop and listen carefully to hear what is behind the words so I don't get trapped into a negative reaction by a manner of expression that is different from mine.

Reality Check Four: People Need to Be True to Themselves

People are not always acting off the wall when we think they are; they are simply being true to themselves. Healthy people are the ones who express themselves without fear, even as they are respectful of the rights of others. They seek to get along, but in the process they stand up for what they believe and do not allow themselves to be run over or crushed.

A young woman shared with a group healthy insight that can be broadened to cover many issues in life. "We live in the same town as my family. They want to eat with us every Sunday, but some weeks I say no! It may be because of schedule conflicts. It may be because we are tired. It may be we just don't want to get together that week."

It is not necessary for us to accept every opportunity offered to us or feel bad if we decline, even with family. Saying no is as important as saying yes. But it is wise to think about how we communicate our acceptance or rejection of ideas, even as we stay true to ourselves. Likewise, when we reject or accept something, we must own our choice. It isn't necessary to justify ourselves to anyone else; it is necessary to be true to ourselves.

Reality Check Five: Know Where Responsibility Ends

Many difficult people enter adulthood with tremendous emotional deficits and unmet needs. Emotionally they are still children—hungry, needy, afraid. These people have a low self-esteem and do whatever is necessary to protect themselves from being hurt again. Either they become overbearing—omnipotent, omniscient, and omnipresent—or they are victims who constantly cry for help or they are rebels, rejecting anything that others want to do for them.

These people have a way of pulling us in and making us respond to them in the way they want. This is the point when we must think about where our responsibility ends. We can put up with someone's demands but not if meeting those demands affects our own self-esteem or intrudes on our other responsibilities. We can lend a helping hand, but we are not responsible for picking someone up and standing that person on his feet. We can be patient with the rebel but also feel free to say that's enough if our efforts are continually rejected.

When we realize where our responsibility ends, it frees us from guilt. We don't have unreasonable expectations for our efforts to help the difficult person, and we are free to get on with our own life.

Different but Okay

Following a grief seminar, an elderly man spoke with me. His only child, a sixty-five-year-old son, had died from a heart attack. He and his wife came to the conference hoping to find help that could ease their grief. After the meeting the man stood with his hat in his hand, looked at me sadly, and said, "Thank you so much for talking about the differences between how men and women grieve. I have not understood my wife." I was amazed. Before me was a man who had to have been married almost seventy years—and he did not understand his wife.

The good news is he was searching for answers. *He did not want to change his wife; he wanted to understand her.* That's what seventy years of living with someone had taught him—not to waste time trying to change someone who is different. Marriage partners so often want to become one, one mind, one heart, one path. Sounds good, but it is really tragic. When two become one, one is lost. The goal in any relationship should be for two to be two, as they walk together. That's growth! Appreciating the differences in people around us expands and enlarges our world.

> Don't waste time trying to change "different"— appreciate it.

I was at a party where two hundred helium-filled balloons were released into the blue Virginia sky. Within seconds the balloons were scattered across the sky, some of them rising hundreds of feet. Some drifted away as far as the eye could see; others were caught in branches and other obstacles nearby. *How interesting!* I thought. *And how similar to people!* Some people soar. They catch the breezes, fly through the skies, seem to be at ease with the height. Some fly closer to the ground. Others cling to the limbs and hang dangerously close to the sharp points.

It's encouraging to know that those who seem to fly so close to the ground can share with their world tales of their flight and visions that have been completely missed by those high in the sky. Those who fly high have visions to share that only they can see. And even those in the branches have an interesting perspective to share. I urge you not to be discouraged if those around you are flying at different heights. Their experiences are preparing them for their own unique journey. It's when those up high talk with and enjoy those down low and vice versa that we all benefit. No height is best, no view superior. They are just different. And when shared, they expand all of our horizons. Different isn't wrong as long as it isn't harmful; different is a wonderful opportunity to see the world through someone else's eyes.

Lifelines

- Different doesn't have to be wrong.
- Don't waste time trying to change "different"—appreciate it.

17

When You Want to Help

Help isn't doing it for someone; it's holding a hand while he or she does it.

If you are a friend or family member of someone who is messing up his life and possibly throwing away his potential, it's not only hard to stand by and just watch the desiccation, it is wrong. It's important to touch others with concern and caring when an outside perspective might jump-start some healthier choices. And even though it's a no-brainer that the best help may flow from someone who is emotionally healthy, few of us have it all together all the time, and if we wait until we do, it may be too late to buoy up someone about whom we care.

So what should we do when we are unsure of whether our help will be appreciated or viewed as an intrusion? What is helpful and what makes the situation worse? Which feelings should you trust—the ones that urge you to do what you can or the ones that question the presumptuousness of barging in with suggestions for change?

Available, eager, you search for possible ways to help, encourage, and inspire. You don't want to be seen as a busybody or do something inappropriate, but you are concerned. Your experience says there are right and wrong ways to help. You have watched friends—or a parent—who jumped in too fast with too much and destroyed the fragile lines that held a relationship together. You know some who gave with strings that crippled. You witnessed others who withdrew their support, and the person, who might have made it with a little extra help, collapsed.

To complicate the issue, the choices the person is making affect you or someone about whom you care. Few people are islands in the world. What your SUP does affects you and threatens your world. What he does hurts you or makes you angry. There may be someone else involved that you need to protect. You fear impending disaster. You don't want to tell anyone how to live his life, but what he chooses affects your world too.

Why Helping Is Dangerous

An SUP is like a whirlpool. His neediness pulls you in. The more you give, the more he wants, until you begin to drown. Or the opposite may be true. The more you try to give, the more resistant he is to accepting the help. His short bursts of apparent recovery keep you hanging on, but they don't last. You feel caught in the turmoil.

It's no wonder people question whether they should stay away and let the difficult person work out his own problems. Helping is like walking through a minefield where the slightest wrong step sets off all kinds of explosions. If you are forced to intervene in a crisis, your reward is resentment. If your help fails to bolster up the person in need, you feel guilty. If you sacrificed for someone who blew his opportunity, you may feel angry. If the receiver feels demeaned by the gift, you are branded a controller. If you cross the fine line of privacy, you are viewed with suspicion and fear. If you allow emotions to drive you toward an easy solution, dependency mushrooms and twists the relationship into an unhealthy mix.

Even so, this may be your opportunity to make a difference. Don't be afraid to help but ground yourself in reality. The person you want to change may never change, not in your lifetime, not in his. It takes years to become screwed up, and it takes years—if it ever happens—to unscrew the patterns that have become intrinsic. Your help may not turn the person around; you may be just picking up the pieces. But, of course, it is possible that your help is just what is needed for your SUP to have victory over screwed-up behavior.

When Is Help Help?

I attended a conference led by three speakers. The point of the first speech was: Help by listening. The second speaker told the story of her daughter being murdered in her own driveway by hired killers as her grandson watched. Her speech was spell-binding as she described how her faith brought her peace. After the two talks a mother sitting beside me broke down. One month before, her only son had committed suicide. She cried, "I came to this conference to get help. I know listening is helpful, but all my friends listen. I need to know what to do to survive. Is something wrong with

me that I don't have enough faith to feel at peace about my
son's death? I feel like I am going crazy." Fortunately, the
third speaker answered her question and stated an important
truth that those giving help need to appreciate.

He said, "Listening helps to validate emotions and allow
steam to vent. Faith assures you God has a purpose. But
unless you appreciate what is going on in your emotions
and how they affect your chemicals, your thought processes,
your ability to sleep, your physical health, you will not
recognize the crucial steps needed to move through the
emotions that follow any life difficulty. The confusion will
feel like failure, failure to stand, to feel at peace, to overcome. Find someone who will listen but then will guide you
through the grief process—not someone who tells you how
to get through the maze or criticizes your efforts. You need
education about what is happening to your emotions and
how choices affect the long term. Difficult relationships,
people, and challenges prevent you from seeing the light
through the trees. Your need is for someone who points
the direction, even as he encourages you to listen for God's
still, small whispers."

His point caused me to reminisce about the three physicians
who advised us about our daughter LeeAnne's prognosis—
imminent death. Our six-year-old child died in her father's
arms in the hospital, surrounded by doctors who had just
examined her, finding no indications of anything other than
a flu-like illness. Her death was the result of a viral menin-
gitis. The medical team restarted her heart, put a screw into
her head to relieve the brain swelling, and stabilized her on
a ventilator and other medical paraphernalia. My husband,
Paul, returned to work, believing that she might get worse
and he needed to see as many patients as possible before this
happened. (Denial keeps one from seeing reality.)

Three doctors, knowing it was unlikely that they could keep LeeAnne alive, shared their knowledge and concern. All were friends; all cared; all understood the realities; only one got through our fog. The first physician said, "Betty, LeeAnne is brain dead. If she survives, she will be a vegetable. She will never talk, walk, or in any way communicate. She will be deaf and blind. She will curl into the fetal position. Nothing can be done." My wall went up. I thought, No way! You don't know LeeAnne's perseverance, our determination, God's possibilities.

The second physician called my husband at his office. He knew LeeAnne probably had only a few more hours of life, even hooked up. He said, "Paul, things don't look very good." Do you think Paul got the message that he should drop whatever he was doing and hurry to the hospital? Paul answered, "I know. They really don't." And he began to work even harder, so if things did get worse he would be as free from obligations as it was possible for him to be.

The third physician, Dr. Boyce Berry, shone a light into our darkness. Tears welled in his eyes, "Betty, we've done everything we know to do. The machinery is not holding LeeAnne. She is slipping away. I've been awake all night. I don't think there is any more that can be done." Dr. Berry was quiet, involved, caring, but most of all, he didn't hit me over the head with a sledgehammer of the negative, nor did he paint a neutral picture. He told the truth—the outcome was no longer in the hands of the physicians.

LeeAnne was dying and our family needed to hold her and glean comfort from each other. "LeeAnne, you are going to be all right," we whispered as we said our good-byes.

No one sees through the fog clearly when all the worst realities and prognoses hit him squarely like a fist to the face. Denial blocks the vision. No one sees a light if his own thoughts are merely echoed. In the dark searching, we need someone to quietly turn on a light so that together we can walk out of the fog.

You may have the opportunity to help someone out of a relationship quandary. You can turn on the light if you remember that the best help is help that educates and guides—not giving directions, but laying out the possibilities.

Successful help:

- lends insight and objectivity to the decision-making process
- is grounded in respect
- encourages and supports
- expresses hope
- discourages codependency
- listens and guides
- develops interdependency (healthy support for each other)

Healthy help says, "With a little encouragement you can make it." Help that injures says, "You could never do this on your own." Sometimes the needed help is assurance that mistakes are not the end of the world or that making bad choices is not an inherited trait. Caring doesn't hurt; it feels good even as it encourages someone to make the long-term decision rather than go for the short-term gratification. Loving help nourishes the person's emotional well-being, providing the little boosts necessary to plug along.

When you care, you are there so that the one you care for does not crash and burn. You may be able to help keep the small hurdles from becoming major obstacles. A friend's mother could not settle the choice between several nursing homes. One home was perfect except for the food. The daughter talked through the pros and cons with her mother and in kindness said, "Mom, you like everything else about this home except the food. So if that is the only problem, then perhaps this is your best choice. You don't like the food anywhere."

How Help Becomes Unhealthy

The wrong kind of help is worse than no help at all and can be detrimental to you as well as to the recipient. This help:

- has the potential of drawing you into the fray
- may cripple the other person even further if you give too much
- may make you feel guilty that you can't prevent disaster
- offers a quickie fix that complicates the problem and recovery for the long term

> The wrong kind of help is worse than no help at all.

- lacks honesty or integrity
- shelters someone from the responsibility and consequences of her actions
- rushes in time and again to fix the same problem
- makes you feel frustrated, used, boxed in, and you may begin to wonder if anything you do makes any difference at all

A graduate student asked, "Do you think you could advise me? I have a friend who has messed up his life big-time on drugs and alcohol. He partied all the time, then dropped out of school and married. I've been his only friend through his ups and downs. He saw he was messing up his life so he stopped the drugs, but his wife had married a party guy so she left him. Now he's depressed and addicted. I told him about a trip I am taking this summer to the home of a roommate from Ireland. I did not have the courage to tell him he couldn't come along when he asked to join us. He will be a disaster. My friend has put me between a rock and a hard place."

This young man was blaming his friend for his predicament. He was in a kick-the-donkey cycle because he couldn't say no! Lots of us kick "donkeys"—obstinate people who are unwilling to change course. They infect and affect us by their irregular behavior as they repeat patterns of destructive behavior.

I suggested to the student that he speak with candor to his friend, lay out the problem, listen to his protestations, but firmly say, "I care about you, but because of your problem with drugs, it would be unwise for you to come with us to Ireland—for your sake and for the sake of my roommate and his family."

He chose *not* to talk with his friend, nor to go on the trip, rather than subject himself to the possibility of his friend being angry or breaking off the relationship. Who had control of whom? *Donkeys are rarely given the credit they deserve.* They are smart enough to get what they want—our attention, money, care, pity, whatever it is that they target by their no-budge stance. It seems that in many ways this student, coping with his friend's inappropriate behavior, was the one who has become mule-headed, unable to see how his choices were making things worse.

If you are helping a friend or family member who keeps repeating the same pattern of destructive or manipulative behavior, be careful. Most often the donkey achieves what he wants, because the helper fails to distance himself enough to stay out of the emotional cycle. Addictive behavior isn't the only kind of destructive behavior. It could be an overbearing, demanding parent who commands his adult daughter to come live with him, a child who won't leave home, a friend who abuses your friendship. Whatever your particular situation, ask yourself: Am I doing anything to encourage this person to change? If you want something to be different, you must do something differently or the patterns become locked.

> If you want something to be different, you must do something differently.

When our motivation is saving someone, somehow keeping him from bearing the consequences of his actions, we are creating an unhealthy dependency. When parents try to prevent every bump and bruise, they cripple their child who begins to fear walking on his own. The same holds true for your reaching out to help someone—do it gingerly, as you encourage steps toward independence.

Helping to Protect

Sometimes you must help to protect. You may need to intervene when the power balance is skewed. Long-term destructive patterns can so damage a person's esteem that she is captive to her own pernicious behavior or becomes a willing victim. Help encourages the breaking of negative cycles. Possibly, help will be an intervention that pulls the person out of the fire until she can stabilize.

Help isn't always welcome, nor accepted. If you have experienced pleading unsuccessfully with an adult child not to return to an abusive lifestyle, you know the pain of watching someone destroy his own life. Perhaps your tears and pleading fall on the deaf ears of a daughter who determines to marry a disaster-about-to-happen. Some have loved ones who freely return to cults from which they have been rescued. Still, don't let the failures stop your offering help. Though some won't make it, others will.

It is inappropriate to try to protect everyone from every problem or to correct every mistake. A priest wisely said, "I used to defend my flock from the wolves, until I learned that they were looking to others to stand up for them, rather than standing up for themselves. I now back off and let them take the heat, unless it is heavily unbalanced. How else are they going to learn to handle difficult people and know what it feels like if they do likewise to others?"

Is the relationship heavily unbalanced? Do what you can. At a T-ball game a mother in front of me was so out of control, I feared for her two daughters. The four-year-old was trying desperately to quiet the baby as the mother screamed and shook the kids. Fear was written clearly over both children's faces. I knew if I confronted the mother, she might beat the children to death in the privacy of her home, so I moved gradually to the mother's side. I began talking to her quietly, "Which child is yours on the field? . . . My, you have your hands full, but you are obviously doing a good job. They are precious. . . . My kids are a little older, but I can remember how tired I used to feel." The woman, who was not sure about the intrusion at first, began to soften and allowed me to play with the baby, who did stop crying. She was a stranger. I never saw her again. I know I didn't stop the potential future dangers, but who knows what a soft, caring word might prevent, especially if you can be there for the long haul?

Children in orphanages used to visit families during the Christmas holiday. Forty years after a teenager visited in the home of his Christmas family, he wrote this in a letter:

I will never forget being in your home for that one short week at Christmas. It changed my life. I decided that week that I wanted a home like yours where the kids have a good time and the parents love their children. I did not know homes like that existed before the visit. . . . I hope you will come see my family sometime if you are nearby.

Tough on the Heart

Healthy help comes from the heart, not as a maneuver to gain, but as a gift. It's tough to stand by and watch when you know the negative consequences of a decision, but sometimes there is no other option. Criticism turns off hearing. Threats fall on deaf ears. Love and encouragement offer the strongest hope. A simple comment that can help someone see the truth may be the best help of all. A couple struggling with guilt after their son's suicide said the comment that helped them overcome the horrendous guilt they felt was made by a mere acquaintance: "It was not your choice. It was your son's choice that took his life."

True, but we want to believe we can prevent someone's collapse. We cling to the belief that if we hold someone up long enough, he will get strong, but strength develops as one stands on his own. Too much support causes codependency, spinning off each other, unable to separate without one, or both, crashing. He weakens to the point he can no longer stand on his own.

A couple shared with me a life experience that illustrates graphically the art of healthy help. Their daughter had lupus, a connective tissue disease that required a great deal of medication and professional care. She desperately wanted to go away to college, rather than go to the local community college, so after much soul-searching, they let her spread her wings and fly the several hundred miles away. There were ups and downs, but basically she did well. In her junior year she sought to stretch her boundaries even farther, as she asked her parents' permission to spend the summer in China at an outpost Red Cross center. The parents grappled with their fears and the potential life-threatening dangers—germs, no hospitals, safety, and so on. "It took such courage I thought we wouldn't be able to allow her to go," her father admitted. "Her mother literally vomited the whole week after we took Cindy to the airport to fly to Beijing. But we knew that, though there was a chance she might not make it back, there was a greater chance she would, and if she did, she would be free to live her life to its fullest, feeling capable and able, instead of handicapped and sickly. We had a choice: Tie her to our apron strings for her safety or free her to fly for her life."

Isn't that also your choice? You can hold on to the difficult person and make him dependent, or you can restrain your fears and encourage his flight. There is no magic formula. Your help may make a significant difference; it may not. But don't forget that the wrong kind of help may be worse than no help at all. Remember, healthy help says several things clearly:

> I'm here if you need me.
>
> I'm here even if you choose unwisely.
>
> I'm here, but there are limits and boundaries.
>
> I'm here to encourage you.
>
> I'm here to be an objective sounding board.
>
> I'm here, but I know your choices—and their consequences—belong to you.
>
> I'm here, but I'm willing to lose the relationship if keeping it means we become twisted together.

Seeing Relationships as Gifts

Freedom to give the right kind of support comes when you recognize that a relationship is a gift. People like or dislike you because of their choice to like or dislike you. Your setting of limits and boundaries will not cause your screwed-up person to stop liking you, unless he was merely using you. In reality, your limits may cause him to respect you.

> A healthy relationship is a gift, not dependent on what you give or don't give.

I asked the graduate student I mentioned earlier, "Do you like your friend, despite his boozing and drugs and all the chaos he causes in your life?"

He answered, "Yes, we've been friends a long time." He paused and then drew the conclusion I hoped he would: "The best part of my relationship is that I have learned from watching my friend what I don't want to do with my life. I am learning to not feel responsible to make his life good for him. He has to quit shutting the door on his own foot. And, if I like him, regardless of what he does or doesn't do, that is how he should like me—or else it is not a very good friendship."

When You Need Outside Help

Difficult people may appear to know what they want, not care what you think, and be intent on doing their own thing without regard to others, but as their relationships twist and the challenges of life throw obstacles into their course, often they begin to seek help. If you are coping with a difficult person, you need support too. Join a church, recreation/ exercise center, a club, or a service group to be with others.

The Yellow Pages for 800/900 numbers offer toll-free lines to almost any kind of intervention or private and group counseling service needed.

An outsider—a mentor, a friend, or a professional counselor with an objective view—may help you sort through the feelings, see your way through the obstacle course, share a bit of insight, and encourage you to continue or discontinue. Choose wisely. Counselors are people with their own personal biases. Consider the age, sex, race, and religious bias of the person with whom you would relate most comfortably. But, keep in mind, the most important person in the arena of problem solving is the person who has a problem and wants to find a solution, not the outsider. If you are intent on finding a solution, you are well on your way to achieving that goal.

Select the style of counseling. Some people feel at ease in a group with others who have a common experience and similar stories that may encourage; yet groups can be harmful if the focus is on rehashing the problem and one-upmanship in telling stories of mistreatment rather than seeking resolution. Being a victim can become a hobby.

Some people seek one-on-one counseling where trust is often easier to establish. But one person, professional or friend, is just that—one person, with an agenda, goals, and set ways of working.

If you decide on joint counseling for you and your difficult person, suggest to him that you go together for counseling to learn techniques that will build your relationship. The purpose of counseling is to find out what *you* are doing right and wrong, not how the other guy is wrong. The goal is to find ways to team together. Warning: Seeking outside counsel is of no use if the sessions are just opportunities to criticize.

So go to a counselor and ask:

Is what I feel crazy?
How can I overcome my feelings so I find solutions?
What is normal?
Are my actions/reactions helping or hampering?
How do I become proactive?
How long should I continue on in this situation?

Partnering

The best kind of help is a partnership where people work together, side by side. Though that seems impossible in a difficult relationship, if you keep focused on the goal; refuse to be drawn into the fray; do right, even if the other person does not; and make sure that sincere caring undergirds your actions, you may be surprised by the changes that are possible.

Partnering is not easy, but you can do it if you stop:

- wondering what someone is going to think of you
- thinking you have to have the best or only solution
- fearing your emotions
- believing rejection of your ideas is rejection of you
- feeling threatened
- dreading rejection

A healthy relationship is like a dance with the partners dancing to the same music. They form a team, and their footwork and moves are coordinated to make the dance flow. Partnering, encouraging each other, and showing mutual support are the underpinnings of such a relationship. A dance partner cannot be the orchestra conductor. If a partner becomes the conductor, the dance is no longer a mutual effort. The "conductor" takes over, and his or her partner simply waits to be told how to feel the music.

Dancing as partners—a healthy relationship—allows both people to be individuals. When either party counts on the other to conduct his life, the relationship is a losing proposition. You may be locked in a twisted dance that has encouraged dependency, rather than interdependency, from the beginning of your relationship. Fortunately, the pattern of your dance can change if you decide to do something about it. Healthy relationships don't just happen; you make them happen through right choices, hard work, and determination.

Dance? Even a civil conversation with your SUP may be a challenge. If so, try admiration. What is it you admire in your SUP? Focus on that. Tell him again and again—face-to-face, via letter, or through a greeting card. The seeds of change grow best when they are set in the ground that is tilled by one's choices, rained on by acceptance, and warmed by the sunshine of possibilities. The one thing people who are difficult cannot resist over the long term is caring help that offers hope. True change is the result of a personal choice that flows most easily when the person feels accepted for who he is and appreciates the possibilities to be more. Even a rock can be chiseled away by the soft patter of raindrops.

Lifelines

- The wrong kind of help is worse than no help at all.
- If you want something to be different, you must do something differently.
- A healthy relationship is a gift, not dependent on what you give or don't give.

18

See the Possibilities

Faith sees the possible in the impossible and finds
hope in the hopeless.

Strong faith can be a stabilizing force in the midst of chaotic, difficult relationships, but faith that is out of balance or in the wrong thing can exacerbate the chaos. Having faith that you are here for a purpose, that your mistakes are not fatal, and that difficulties as well as successes provide learning opportunities helps you make the necessary choices for self-control when dealing with off-the-wall people. Healthy faith encourages self-respect as it stabilizes priorities on a solid foundation. With faith, your choices are rooted in a long-term vision, which allows you to be flexible so that you can withstand the short-term storms. Healthy faith helps you find solutions and peace, even as you cope with difficult people.

If faith is skewed and out of balance, people may become embroiled in unhealthy interactions that tear them apart. For instance, a young man frantically described himself as being on the brink of losing his mind because of the war between his mother and his wife that put him in the middle of their dogfights. He was experiencing an undeniable faith crisis that kept him fence-sitting. He clung to one mandate of Scripture without balancing it with others. "What am I to do? My faith says I am to honor my parents." Did he not know that Scripture also says, "Leave your mother and father and cling to your wife" (see Eph. 5:31)?

A young woman telephoned me. "Help! I think I'm going crazy! Three months ago I found our eight-month-old son dead in his crib from sudden infant death syndrome." She was floundering in faith misunderstandings. "My minister says I should rejoice because I have the assurance my baby is in heaven," she said. Not only did she not feel joy, she was burdened with guilt from having aborted her first child. She asked, "Do you believe my first baby is in hell? Could God be punishing me?"

This young woman did not understand the tough emotions of grief any more than the young man recognized that his blind, unbalanced adherence to one tenet of his faith kept him from establishing the right line of loyalty. Both of these people were struggling because faith done wrong seems useless and just wishful thinking. Such faith misunderstandings cause doubts that are expressed in statements such as these: I wouldn't feel like this if I had enough faith . . . If I truly forgave, I would forget . . . I wouldn't fly off the handle if I loved enough.

> Faith done wrong makes your relationships sick.

Faith Answers the "Why"

When we struggle with relationship problems, we have a lot of *whys*. They rain on us constantly. Why do I have to put up with this? Why am I treated so poorly? Why don't I just leave? We grapple to find the peace religious clichés espouse. We long for a faith like the child who attended the prayer service in Iowa where drought had parched and browned the fields, and the crops lay wilting from thirst. Local ministers called for an hour of prayer on the town square, asking everyone to bring an object of faith for inspiration. The townspeople filled the square with anxious faces and hopeful hearts, a variety of objects clutched in prayerful hands—holy books, crosses, rosaries. When the hour ended, as if on command, a soft rain began to fall. Cheers swept the crowd as they held their treasured objects high in gratitude and praise. One faith symbol seemed to overshadow all the others: A nine-year-old child had brought an umbrella.[1] We long to have hope in seemingly hopeless relationships and believe the impossible is possible, as did this little girl.

I have purposefully placed this chapter on faith at the end of the book because I want to emphasize that each of us is responsible for choices that will bring healing to damaged relationships, and what we believe affects those choices. Too many people try religion and find their faith does not shield them from problems, so they decide that their religion is worthless and decry faith's inability to change the troublesome person in their life or prevent the chaos. Others, burdened by sorrows and challenges, cocoon themselves in religion, driving others away by their piety. Yet if we reject faith because some people are out of balance and cause us continual heartache, we are neglecting the very element that is needed for peace within difficult relationships. We are stabilized when in us the four elements that battle for mind control work in sync: emotions, attitudes, physical nature, and spiritual nature.

The director of a national grief recovery group, in her introductory remarks before the weekend seminar assembly, said, "In our organization we never talk about religion." She was attempting to solve the problem of pie-in-the-sky solutions to real-life problems by disallowing any discussion of this vital area of all human life. Wrong choice. Victorious living is dependent on head-to-head combat with the questions that beg to hold us captive, and the armor we need for the battle is a healthy faith in God.

I was the speaker for that seminar and knew that the seminar would fail to meet crucial needs if we did not address questions that swirled around faith. The spiritual dimension is a crucial part of who we are. To deny that dimension leaves people feeling empty, like something is missing or being ignored. Spiritual issues are more basic than denominational or religious preference. They are the issues the young mother battled, "Did God zap me?" They are the issues raised by Rabbi Kushner in his book *When Bad Things Happen to Good People*.[2] Spiritual issues are the *why* issues. Why did this happen?

People are confused by faith that promises anything is yours for the asking when their experience seems to show that their prayers go unanswered. Doubts arise when time after time returning good for evil has no positive effect in a bad relationship, and broken commitments and life crises continue. They often come to one or several of the following conclusions:

- their faith was not strong enough
- their prayers not good enough

- their sin too bad to be forgiven
- their suffering necessary for purification

Perhaps you have lost heart and you struggle with faith issues because of overwhelming and frustrating difficulties in crucial relationships. Your efforts to change irrational and erratic behavior in someone to whom you feel committed or duty bound to help is driving you away from belief. You feel cursed, not blessed. What good is believing in a God who does not eliminate your problems—or at least grant you peace within the difficult situations? Basing your loyalties and commitment on rules that seem to reinforce pandemonium goes against your screaming emotions. When embroiled and embittered relationships drive you away from faith, what are you to do?

Faith Forms a Solid Ground

Let us look together at the benefits of a grounded, balanced faith. Recognition of the value of a living faith can encourage you to seek real answers to the why questions, rather than allowing chaotic emotions to control your thoughts. God does not resolve all our problems, but he does offer to be with us as we work through them. Faith teaches:

My life has purpose.
I'm not in this alone.
The circumstances in my life are not a mistake (nor are the people).
My mistakes are not fatal.
Relationship difficulties are opportunities for growth.

> Healthy faith opens your eyes to the gifts and opportunities.

These understandings turn our windshield wipers on so that we can clearly see that our unique assets are not dependent on affirmation by our SUP. Such faith undergirds us with a power to give to others and overcome challenges without feeling that we are unworthy unless our gifts are adequately acknowledged and appreciated. We stand without fear on our beliefs, and we are able to help or walk away without guilt. We are able to feel sorrow for the weakness, failure, need for control, or inability to relate exhibited in our SUP's life. We turn the negative challenges in the relationship into opportunities to love in spite of everything. Healthy faith can change our perspective and free us to see relationship challenges as opportunities for us to make a difference.

Faith Changes the Perspective

A father shared his experience with me: "I remember sitting on the couch in my living room after my teenage son was killed in a motorcycle accident. His life was over like a whiff. Here today, laughing and being all boy; gone tomorrow. The silence was deafening. Tears that were too heavy to fall filled my insides and simply spilled over. I survived the three days between death and burial by focusing on how blessed my life had been by such an enthusiastic, capable son and how blessed he had been to have supportive family and friends who helped him believe in himself. He was born without a foot, but because so many people encouraged him, he never thought of himself as handicapped.

"As I reminisced, two people whose critical spirits and negative behaviors drove me bonkers popped into my mind.

Those two people, like my son, were handicapped, but instead of encouraging them and affirming their strengths, I pounded on their failures and weaknesses to make them change. They were far from perfect, but, then, so was my son!"

In reality this father's son was handicapped, but he was not a cripple, because people encouraged his strengths as they made allowances for his missing foot. I

> Envisioning your screwed-up person as handicapped changes your perspective.

have found this to be a most effective way of turning around negative thoughts about screwed-up people. Dwelling on the strengths does not blind me to the weaknesses, but it does help me feel sorry instead of angry at the offensive behaviors.

In truth, a screwed-up person is handicapped. Her problem isn't a missing limb or a disease. If it were, people would be more merciful than they are to those with hurtful, irregular behaviors. People tend to forgive ugly moods, agitation, and whining that is the by-product of disease or crisis, but they are merciless with those handicapped by negative behaviors that just seem to be part of the person's personality. By turning your anger at aberrant behavior into pity, you free yourself from the stranglehold the difficult person has over your emotions. Criticism, like anger, may become habitual but is ineffective in bringing about change. Allowing God to refocus your vision on a person's strengths and neediness empowers you to hang in there, rather than giving up, when the going is tough.

Faith Helps Meet the Challenge

Overcoming the negative pull of toxic people can seem as impossible as climbing Mount Everest. The longer the climb, the less oxygen fills your lungs. You struggle as the conflict patterns continue, feeling you can't breathe. Your muscles scream out in pain for lack of oxygen. You feel hope being squeezed from your soul. Continuing on, even one six-inch step at a time, requires tremendous strength. Yet you can stand—as did Edmund Hillary, the first man to climb Mount Everest—pointing toward your mountain and declaring in a loud voice, "You beat me the first time, but I'll beat you the next because you've grown all you are going to grow, but I'm still growing." One year after facing his challenge, Edmund Hillary made his successful climb.

> Climbing over mountainous relationship obstacles starts one step at a time.

Undergirded by a faith that helps you see the impossible as possible, you can be successful in separating yourself from the disheartening pull of a toxic relationship—if not on the first try, then on the next or the next. Faith turns failures and challenges in toxic relationships into stepping stones, growth points. The trials take on meaning as they become opportunities to overcome the "mountain" and, through the process, offer hope to others who are making the climb.

It's not how long it takes to overcome the mountain of obstacles in your relationship that is important; it's finally feeling in control of yourself, regardless of the dysfunction of the other guy.

Faith Takes Risks

There's a story about two seeds that lay side by side in the fertile spring soil. The first seed said, "I want to grow and send my roots deep into the soil beneath me and thrust my sprouts through the earth's crust above me. I want to feel the warmth of the sun on my face and the refreshing morning dew on my petals." And so she grew. The second seed said, "I'm afraid. If I send my roots into the ground below, I may bump into rocks or bugs. It will be dark and damp. If I push my way through the hard soil above me, I may damage my delicate sprouts. I will wait until it is safe." And so she waited. In the early spring, a bird scratching around for food found the waiting seed and promptly ate it.[3]

Screwed-up people, like the bird, will swallow your joy, destroy your relationships, and leave you floundering in doubts about your self-worth if you lie around waiting for the other guy to change. You must risk changing old patterns. Prayer can help you do that. Prayer makes the roots of faith dig down deep and hold tight. Studies at Duke University have shown the amazing power of prayer to cause change. Prayer works. It works on the person who prays, in particular. Pray for someone and your anger abates, regardless of what the person does not do.

Prayer balances out the power struggle in difficult relationships, because when you have a relationship with God, you are no longer so vulnerable or reactive.

> Faith isn't about the other guy; it's always about me.

Prayer helps you talk out the *whys*. It helps you grow an acorn of concern into an oak tree of strength that holds you and those you care about up through the storms. Prayer is a spiritual tool that shuts *your* mouth and opens *your* heart.

Faith isn't about the other guy. It's always about me. It's my roots that must go down deep or, regardless of what someone else does, I am the one who gets gobbled up. Faith empowers me to take the risks. It's a risk to move toward change, but in relationships, like all of nature, nothing stays the same.

Here is the hard and fast rule of relationships: Degeneration is inevitable unless one risks choices and makes the effort to move toward positive change.

Faith Finds the Good

Faith is seeing that God can turn even the tragic into ways to reach out and touch others, even as he heals the wounds. After the publication of my first book, *Sunrise Tomorrow: Coping with a Child's Death*, I was asked to speak in conferences across the country on handling grief, in particular grief caused by the death of a child. I understood what families were going through and had advice to give, but during those first few months of helping others, I was flooded with piercing memories. I came home from speaking engagements emotionally exhausted. The day I determined to stop, I laid out my plan and then repeated it all day long. I talked long and hard to God, "No more. I've done my part to help. It's too painful and I'm so tired. My family and I need to move into more joyful arenas."

That very night my husband handed me a letter that had been delivered to his office. It was from a young mother in Illinois. She was poised to commit suicide when she decided to look through a copy of *Sunrise Tomorrow*, given to her by a friend. "It was like lightning hit me. . . . Someone who thought there was no way to go on, just like I did, found ways to survive." She realized that what she was experiencing was normal. She was not crazy. Others had made it through the pain. Perhaps she could also. Let me share some of her seven-page, handwritten letter:

> . . . I was so weary, discouraged, and hopeless. My husband was my life. We had tried so hard to have

children—and now we had a seven-year-old son and a two-year-old daughter. With everything going for us, he left to fling with his secretary. I hurt inside and out.

My folks were the only ray of hope. They kept us afloat financially and picked up the children if work demanded I stay late. It was 9 P.M. when I picked up the children this night. . . . I was dog tired. My little boy got in the backseat and my little girl got in the front, but she was begging, "Please, Momma, let me spend the night with G'ma . . ." over and over . . . so I let her ask.

I slumped down over the steering wheel and wondered how I could make it. I just got lost in my thoughts, and when Mary came back, though I saw and heard her, it was like I was in a fog. All I remember is that the door was swinging shut on her hands. I reached to stop it, but as I did, my foot hit the accelerator, then the brake, the gas, the brake. When I got the car stopped and came around to see how she was, my little boy was standing over Mary, saying, "Why did you kill my sister? Why did you kill my sister?"

I didn't think I could survive the funeral—and then the pain got worse. I didn't want to live . . . but as I read Sunrise Tomorrow, it was like you were saying what I felt. Your little girl died of a virus. You felt the same things I did. If you and the others could make it, maybe I could. I'm all my son has left . . .

My eyes opened. It wasn't a mistake that I had prayed "No way" that particular day. It wasn't a mistake the letter arrived that evening. I couldn't change what had happened. All my longing would not bring my little girl back. All I could do was see the opportunities and blessings that flow from within the good and bad times and share them with others, so that perhaps they would find encouragement to move one foot in front of the other too. Prayer is far less likely to change the other guy than it is to change the person who prays.

Faith Lets You Bend

Author Henri J. M. Nouwen has written a compelling book, *The Return of the Prodigal Son*, based on Rembrandt's painting.[4] At the heart of this book are a seventeenth-century painting and its artist, a first-century parable and its author, and a twentieth-century person in search of life's meaning. Nouwen spins a masterful story of the five people in the painting—the prodigal, the father, the other son, and two onlookers.

I was drawn to the father when I read the book. He is a study of faith in action. Here was a man who was dealing with a rebellious son. Perhaps you are coping with a difficult child. If so, you can probably relate to the feelings this father must have had—frustration, anxiety, anger, guilt, pain. How angry and hurt he must have felt when his son said the unthinkable: "Pop, you're old. I'm young. I need my inheritance while I'm still young enough to enjoy it. I wish you would just go ahead and die—or give it to me anyway."

His father could have refused. Perhaps he was torn between protecting his son, kicking him out of the house with nothing, or giving him the inheritance with a shove and a

"Don't come back!" But, instead, he said, "Here, Son. Take your share. I trust you will use it wisely. Just know you can come home if things don't work out." It takes courage to allow someone you love to face the potential negative consequences of his actions. It takes wisdom to

> Being deeply rooted allows you to bend.

keep the door open. It takes a walk with faith to still love when your emotions scream, *It's not fair!*

It is obvious as you study the parable that, though the father loved his son, he trusted that someone else loved him too. He knew he couldn't protect his son from all the bruises of life if he wanted him to become strong enough to stand alone. Yet his faith consoled him with the assurance that neither he nor his son was in it alone. God was involved. God is involved in your life story too. You are not alone as you struggle for wisdom to do the right thing in your difficult relationship. You don't have to change the person who is driving you nuts. You just have to do the right thing yourself and trust that you aren't the only one who cares about your "handicapped" family member, friend, coworker, boss—or yourself.

Faith Recognizes That I Make a Difference

Two people came up to share their life story with me at the conclusion of a three-hour widowed persons' conference, which ended with a "pep rally"—Rah! Rah! You can do it! I expected an enthusiastic "I've made it!" tale from each of these vivacious senior citizens. But, instead, before me stood night and day—a toxic person who probably dampened most of the relationships around her and a hero of epic proportions who was a beacon of hope to those who knew him.

The widow blurted out a list of "I can'ts" followed by a litany of health problems. Her tale of woe was distressing. What could I say that I had not already said? This was her life, regardless of its limitations. Instead of cherishing the priceless gift of life, she complained about her misfortunes. She relegated herself to a waiting zone, waiting to die.

In contrast, Mr. Brownlow inspired. Stooped by rheumatoid arthritis, barely able to walk, he sparkled with enthusiasm that energized and inspired. As he talked, his twinkling eyes brimmed with tears, "I'm ninety-six years old and have a hard time getting around, but I go as much as I can. I've lost my wife—married sixty-three years—and three sons. One son died when we were working together on power lines in a storm. I really get lonely, but I know I'm supposed to be here or I wouldn't be. I don't have a moment to waste. There are so many people who just need an encouraging call." Mr. Brownlow's faith was alive and well. His life was a lesson in living faith that said, "I see the possibilities." His faith focus was upward instead of inward.

Faith changes you, even as it enables you to encourage, support, uphold, and respect others with whom you have a difficult relationship. Faith also enables you to let go, if necessary, of that relationship. Being deeply rooted nourishes you when the turmoil embroils and exhausts your body, mind, and soul. Faith does help, if it is healthy faith. There's no question: *What you believe will make a difference in the difference you make.*

Lifelines

- Faith done wrong makes your relationships sick.
- Healthy faith opens your eyes to the gifts and opportunities.

- Envisioning your screwed-up person as handicapped changes your perspective.
- Climbing over mountainous relationship obstacles starts one step at a time.
- Faith isn't about the other guy; it's always about me.
- Being deeply rooted allows you to bend.

19

Dancing with Porcupines

Relationships with screwed-up people are like dancing with a porcupine: You want to dance close enough to enjoy the waltz but not so close you end up shot full of quills.

The great ice hockey player Wayne Gretzky was quoted as saying, "I'm not the fastest nor the strongest, but I know how to keep my eye on the puck." In relationships, the possibilities are the puck. Keeping your eye on the possibilities is tricky when you are dancing with a porcupine. It's not impossible, but it takes a lot of sheer willpower to focus on the possibilities when you keep being stuck by the quills. Yet the excitement of a difficult relationship lies in the discovery of the value of someone who hides behind prickly defenses and in affirming your flexibility that helps you bend without breaking. You begin to see your challenging relationship as a small miracle that can bring about knowledge and change to you both. The reality is that if you want relief beyond belief, you must learn to dance with the porcupines.

Regeneration

The canary has powers we can only dream of: Its brain can grow new nerve cells. Neurogenesis, the rebirth of brain nerve cells, is quite common in adult fish, as well as in reptiles and rats. Human brains cannot regenerate nerve cells, but unlike most of nature's other creatures, we are able to continuously reprogram our thoughts. We are able to change, flex, and grow as we respond to challenges. And through our efforts, not only are we strengthened, but we can help someone who is floundering.

You may be in the midst of the fires of a difficult relationship and feel you are about to experience a meltdown. You long for easy, kind, and caring interaction. But you won't have to give up on yourself, and probably not on the relationship either, if you keep focused. Sometimes just remembering that you are dancing with a porcupine keeps you alert but not surprised when you get pricked. If you have decided that the relationship you desire is worth working for, keep making the effort until your goal is achieved. Your effort will be fully productive when you stop holding back in a defensive posture and determine to make the most of the possibilities within your grasp today. Screwed-up relationships teach us to stop thinking in terms of forever. We think of now, a day at a time, knowing forever will take care of itself.

Learn to Dance

It's a comfort to discover that a sad start is precisely that and not necessarily the end of the world. It's not turning your back on what happened that frees you from the hurts of the past; it's refusing to blame the bad in your life on a particular person, it's claiming life with vigor, and it's harnessing the injustice and wrong into life lessons that teach you the preciousness of the kind and the right.

It's natural for young people to feel the pain of a life that's not fair and try to place blame as they thrash out their identity. There comes a time, however, when continuing to blame the problems of your life on others is nonproductive, unhealthy, and a bar to happiness. That's when it is time to come to a more understanding way.

"I broke the pattern of disaster because it wasn't acceptable to me," a middle-aged father said when talking about the curse of an unhappy childhood that had spilled into his own marriage and parenting. "It took almost losing my family to open my eyes to the damage my parents had done. Now that I have stopped blaming my folks and feeling bitter, I see clearly that I don't want to be part of that cycle ever again. The bitterness and anger were affecting my relationship with my wife and children, driving them away. I don't want to do to my children what my parents did to me. They taught me what not to do. Now I realize my life is my choice."

Many people have conquered and overcome the hurts and angers that grew out of an unhappy childhood or problem relationships in their adult years. Charlie Chaplin saw his own mother committed to an asylum. His early life was full of turmoil and emotional pain, but he used his experience to create high comic art tinged with sadness. Tina Turner openly talks about her violent, troubled marriage to Ike. It took time after their divorce before she felt whole again and could continue with her singing career. For many, life is a gutter experience. But in the end it's not where you have been or with what you have started, but, rather, where you go and what you make from your beginnings that can bring you happiness.

Love Openly

One of the tragedies facing relationships today is the crisis of loving left undone, the reluctance to love openly and demonstratively because of the fear of getting hurt. We struggle with daily issues in our interactions, we disagree, and too many of us wait too long to reconcile. We hold back, thinking loving freely doesn't punish someone enough for his failures. We hang back, believing he owes us and we should wait until he pays his debt before we really commit to him. We see the people in our life as full of faults. We can't see any positives. We hang our hat on what is missing, on what we wish was our lot.

You may have made mistakes and wasted a lot of time, as anyone caught in a difficult relationship does. You may have held back from loving openly, but it is never too late to change. In Charles Dickens's *A Christmas Carol*, Scrooge becomes a new man in his old age, filled with energy and zest, transformed after being visited by the three Christmas ghosts. The Broadway musical *Scrooge* focuses on the changes in his life as he redirected his priorities, values, and attitudes. He changed from miserly to generous, miserable to radiantly happy, selfish to caring, a loser to a winner. He showed that to be a winner is not dependent on your having done it right in the past; it depends on your doing it right in the present. Could you apply the message from Scrooge's pivotal song to your life?

I'll begin today and throw away the past. And the future I build will be something that will last.

I will take the time I have left to live and I will give it all I have left to give. . . .

And I will thank the Lord and remember when I was able to begin again.

It Takes Time

Building a whole and healthy relationship is not a linear process. The relationship with your SUP will move forward, slide back, get stuck, and move forward again. The effort can seem overwhelming, but each time you move ahead, you will feel the lightness of freedom urging you on. Expect your efforts to falter; expect to make mistakes as you learn to act and not react. Even when you begin to sense peace within a previously chaotic relationship, you will never be totally free of anxiety, confusion, fear, or guilt. No one is. You will blow it, try again, and blow it again. Be patient as you try. Perhaps you will conclude that the relationship is hopeless. If so, learn from it.

> When we are freed from bondage in a difficult relationship, we, like the angels, fly because nothing holds us down.

Figuring ways to make it work, or accepting the reality that it won't work, is not a waste. These are the growth points, the great grow-up lessons. No matter what, don't give up on seeking good relationships with others. Our trials, pressures, temptations, successes, and failures in relationships chip away our rough edges, shaping us into quality people with the ability to soar and shine in the midst of everything we face. When we are freed from bondage in a difficult relationship, we, like the angels, fly because nothing holds us down.

An elderly man reminisced: "I hope my sons get it together quicker than I did. I've spent most of my life trying to be the top dog with the perfect wife and kids. I was the absolute ruler of my domain. It took my family almost crashing and burning before I saw the picture. I needed to control me.

Whatever time I have left, I intend to spend loving, support-
ing, and encouraging."

This man had to navigate several passages of life before
he became clear-sighted. It probably stung to recognize that
most of the relationship problems in his life were not the
other guy's fault, but his own. He had been the screwed-up
person. Now he was finding that, though he couldn't change
the past, he had the power to
turn his life around and offer
hope to those he had injured.
He learned that happiness is not
something controlled by what
someone else does; you grow it
yourself. You plant it, you nur-
ture it, and you reap it. He found that being thunder, making
great noise, brought nothing but chaos. Love and encouragement, on the other hand, water the fragile seeds of peace
and contentment.

> It's not the noise you make; it's the love and encouragement you give that make your life matter.

A lot can be forgiven in your life, a lot of bad overlooked,
and a lot of mistakes pardoned when people recognize you
have turned your vision from the degrees you earned, positions you held, or wealth you amassed to the people in your
life. Longevity and productivity don't matter the most—they
are not good measures of a life. What matters is who has
loved you, whom you have loved, and how you have loved.
The circle of love is everything.

You Are Responsible

You are responsible for the way your life turns out, not chance,
not someone else. The SUP in your life may make it difficult
for you to focus on what you should be doing with your life.
Stop and resolve: *I will no longer permit the person who has*

consumed so much of my life to have power over any more of it. There's a better way to do it, and I am going to find it!

The purpose of this book is not to lay out a specific plan but to guide you into finding your own path. The way is already in you. All you need to do to follow it is to recognize it and act on it.

Let's review some of the important points of this book that will help you on your way:

- Few people are screwed up in all areas of their life. That's why their behavior is so confusing.
- No one owes anyone anything; a relationship is a gift.
- You may be someone's lifeline, even though it seems to you the tables should be reversed.
- If you focus on a person's failures, you will never see any good to encourage.
- "You should" is one of life's most destructive phrases.
- It's important to have limits and boundaries and let other people know what they are.
- Though your heart may ache for your screwed-up person, it is his own responsibility to stand up and overcome his problems.
- It's crucial to be true to yourself, even as you help where you can.
- You can't protect everyone; you can't stop all the wrong; you can't control someone else.
- There's always a danger of being sucked into dysfunctional behavior.
- If you stay in the relationship, rather than quit, you won't do it all right. But you won't stay stuck either, because your eyes have been opened and you have felt the freedom of soaring above the relationship fray.

- Your future is wide open, and the possibilities are endless.

The most significant question this book has addressed is, Do you want your screwed-up relationship to change? A lot of people answer yes, but what they mean is they want it to work if the other guy will change, if they don't have to forgive, and if they are paid back for all they have lost. As we've seen, that's not the way it works. There are things you must do to make it work, and if it is never what you dreamed of, there are things to do to help you cope and keep you going. If you are ready to do what it takes to make your relationship work or to cope if it doesn't, you may want to take the following pledge: Today, from this moment forward,

I will no longer allow what others do to control how I feel.

I will cease living my life through someone else.

I will appreciate and build on what I have, rather than wishing for something else.

I will find healthy ways to meet my needs, rather than expecting someone else to do it.

I will learn from all of my life—from the bad as well as the good.

I will take advantage of opportunities to grow emotionally, physically, and spiritually.

I will be grateful for each moment.

I will treasure my own value.

Steven Spielberg was interviewed by Barbara Walters, who asked, "If you could change any ending to any movie, which one would it be and how would you change it?"

Spielberg thought a moment and answered, "I would change the ending of *Gone with the Wind* where Rhett Butler looks at his wife and says, 'Frankly, my dear, I don't give a d——!' and walks out. Instead, I'd have him look at Scarlett and do what we all have to do in real life when someone is driving us crazy. He would look straight in her eyes and say, 'Frankly, my dear, I do give a d——! What can we do to get along better?'"

Lifelines

- When we are freed from bondage in a difficult relationship, we, like the angels, fly because nothing holds us down.
- It's not the noise you make; it's the love and encouragement you give that make your life matter.

Notes

Chapter 4 Get Off the Fence

1. Rick Reilly, "Top Hat," *Sports Illustrated* 85, no. 18 (October 28, 1996): 50.
2. Michael J. McManus, *Marriage Savers: Helping Your Friends and Family Stay Married* (Grand Rapids: Zondervan, 1993), 30.

Chapter 6 Heal the Hidden Wound

1. Paraphrase of Dorothy L. Nolte, "Children Learn What They Live," see http://www.EmpowermentResources.com/.
2. Thomas A. Harris, *I'm OK—You're OK* (New York: Avon, 1973).

Chapter 7 Can Ailing Relationships Make You Sick?

1. Norman Cousins, *Anatomy of an Illness Perceived by the Patient: Reflections on Healing and Regeneration* (New York: Norton, 1979).
2. Bernie S. Siegel, *Love, Medicine, and Miracles* (New York: Harper and Row, 1986).
3. McManus, *Marriage Savers,* 29.
4. Ibid., 30–31.
5. Ibid., 31.
6. Ibid.
7. Donald Langsley and David M. Kaplan, *The Treatment of Families in Crisis* (New York: Grune, 1968), 48.
8. Thomas H. Holmes and Richard H. Rahe, "Holmes-Rahe Life Events Test" (1967); see http:www.prcn.org/next/stress.html.

Chapter 9 Let the Past Go

1. Judith S. Wallerstein and Sandra Blakeslee, *Second Chances: Men, Women, and Children a Decade after Divorce* (New York: Tichnor and Fields, 1989), 45.

2. Wayne W. Dyer, *Your Erroneous Zones* (New York: Funk and Wagnalls, 1976), 89.

3. Melody Beattie, *Codependent No More* (San Francisco: HarperSanFrancisco, 1987), 63.

Chapter 10 Buttons and Triggers

1. Joyce Landorf, *Irregular People* (Waco: Word, 1962), 37.

Chapter 11 Make Anger Your Ally

1. Neil Clark Warren, *Make Anger Your Ally* (Colorado Springs: Focus on the Family, 1993).

Chapter 13 How Can I Ever Forgive?

1. John Haggai, *My Son Johnny* (Wheaton: Tyndale, 1978).

Chapter 14 How Many Times Do I Say "Sorry"?

1. Viktor Frankl, *Man's Search for Meaning* (Boston: Beacon, 1963).

Chapter 15 Touch with Words

1. This story is found in David Augsburger, *The Freedom of Forgiveness* (Chicago: Moody, 1970), 107–9.

2. Stephen Covey, *The Seven Habits of Highly Effective People* (New York: Simon and Schuster, 1989), 142.

3. C. Everett Koop in speech at Christian Medical Dental Society Conference, King College, Bristol, Tenn., June 14, 1998.

Chapter 16 Is "Different" Screwed Up?

1. Mark I. Rosen, *Why Are People Difficult?* (Goshen, Ky.: Harmony), 31.

Chapter 18 See the Possibilities

1. Adapted from Laverne W. Hall, in Jack Canfield et al., *Chicken Soup for the Christian Soul* (Deerfield Beach, Fla.: Health Communications), 198.

2. Harold S. Kushner, *When Bad Things Happen to Good People* (New York: Schocken, 1981).

3. Patsy Hanson, Gibson greeting card, adapted from *Chicken Soup for the Soul* .

4. Henri J. M. Nouwen, *The Return of the Prodigal Son* (New York: Continuum, 1995).

Elizabeth B. Brown received her bachelor's degree from Emory and Henry College and her master's degree in psychology and counseling from Virginia Commonwealth University. Betty is a frequent speaker for grief seminars, conferences, and women's religious retreats across the country, including Hospice, Contact, Christian Women's Club, Widowed Person's Association, and Compassionate Friends. She currently teaches a course on death and dying at East Tennessee State University Quillen Medical School. She and her physician husband, Paul, live in Johnson City, Tennessee.

Crazy co-workers stressing you out? Here's the solution.

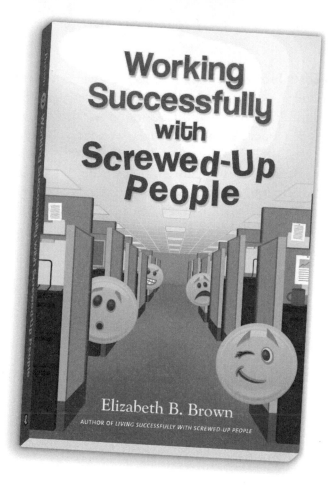

Less stress at work can start today.
So what are you waiting for?

YOU **DON'T** HAVE TO BE CONTROLLED BY **DIFFICULT PEOPLE!**

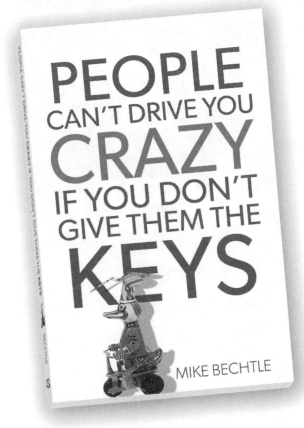

Communication expert Mike Bechtle shows you how to stop being a victim of other people's craziness. With commonsense wisdom and proactive advice that you can put into practice immediately, Bechtle gives you a proven strategy to handle crazy people—and stay sane while doing it.

Make positive changes to improve your life.

"Like the fairy tale suggests, the 'mirror, mirror on the wall' shows us the face of our enemy. . . . We defeat ourselves far more than we are defeated by external circumstances."

—from the foreword by John C. Maxwell

"Read this wise book and skillfully navigate your important conversations." **—Dr. Les Parrott III**

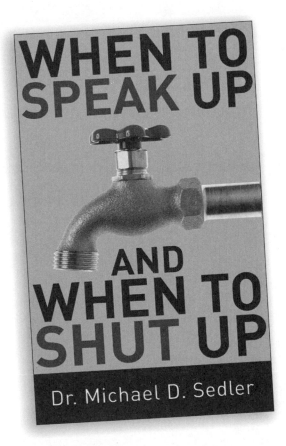

Discover important strategies for building better communication within your workplace, church, and home.

You Can Excel in the Art of Confident Conversation

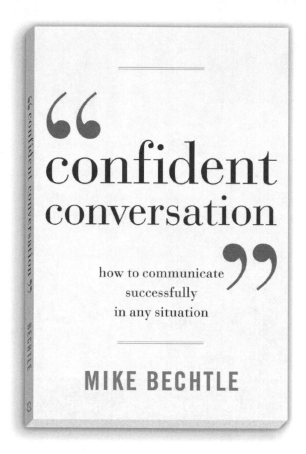

"Does anyone really know how to communicate well? Mike does, and this is a great tool to develop more intimate relationships and deeper connections in any situation."

—Steve Arterburn, New Life Ministries

Revell
a division of Baker Publishing Group
www.RevellBooks.com